T0332131

QUILOMBOLA!

Series Editor

LÉONORA MIANO

Quilombola is a Brazilian word for the inhabitant of a maroon, or 'runaway-slave' community. The choice of this appellation is a tribute to those who, throughout human history, have stood up against oppression. However, there is more in this reference: it speaks both about freedom regained and about all the creative gestures that stemmed from that conquest. For those who had broken their chains, the *quilombo* was a place of reappropriation and reinvention of oneself.

It is by inviting writers and readers to practice *marronnage*—'running away from slavery'—of thought, to shift their way of thinking, that the series **Quilombola!** stands out. This list of books is a space from which resonate insubordinate, inventive, provocative and unexpected voices. Whether artists, activists or intellectuals, the authors of **Quilombola!** bring a sensitive reflection on the world and forge new paths. Although focusing on sub-Saharan African and French-speaking Afropean expressions, we welcome minority points of view from other places too.

The series aims at making itself accessible to a large readership in order to promote a wider circulation of thought. It is on this condition that it will come to meaningful fruition.

Coming Out of My Skin

JEAN-BAPTISTE PHOU

TRANSLATED BY
EDWARD GAUVIN

Seagull
BOOKS

LONDON NEW YORK CALCUTTA

Seagull Books, 2023

Originally written in French
© Jean-Baptiste Phou, 2021

First published in English translation by Seagull Books, 2023
English translation © Edward Gauvin, 2023

ISBN 978 1 8030 9 233 1

British Library Cataloguing-in-Publication Data
A catalogue record for this book is available from the British Library

Typeset by Seagull Books, Calcutta, India
Printed and bound in the USA by Integrated Books International

I

1

You will marry a Chinese girl. I was going on ten when I heard my mother utter those words for the first time. It was the late 1980s. We lived in a house in the suburbs south of Paris: my parents, my three siblings, our two dogs. Those words, which I was to hear all my life—were they a wish? A prediction? A commandment? Or merely well-meaning advice from a mother who wanted the best for her son, a reserved way of saying 'I love you'? *See, even our French neighbour is with an Asian girl: they make the best wives!* Despite leaving China's Chaoshan region for Cambodia generations ago, my mother's family had held on to its language and traditions, and she in turn wished to preserve her cultural heritage. *A Teochew woman would be even better—we'd speak the same language!* The genocidal Khmer Rouge regime had taken her parents and half her siblings, yet my mother, along with a fellow countryman in exile, had made a home and a family for herself in France. *Family is the most important thing there is. You must cherish your family.*

Perhaps my mother had followed a path laid out before her, taking her place among her parents, her grandparents, because it was simply 'in the order of things'? This phrase had a very different ring to me: the imposition of endogamy and a traditional family model, a summons to conformity, an injunction to toe the line.

The child that I was could not see so far into the future. But already, I had a feeling that this was not how things would go for me. Around this time, I became aware I was different. I felt attracted to boys. I couldn't really wrap my head around the sexual—these days we would say 'gendered'—division of chores, games, and clothes in force in my family environment: women in the kitchen and men in the living room, dolls for girls and cars for boys, women in dresses and men in pants. I wanted to roam from room to room, seizing toys or clothes at whim. Among women, I was told to run along. *This is no place for a boy*! Among men, I never felt at ease. Chasing after a ball, braying and brawling. I often wound up alone in a corner, unable to find my place.

I shared a room with my brother, who was two years older. He seemed to move so easily through that world meant for boys. We never had much to say to each other. Most of the time, I would cut myself from the outside world with my Walkman. Music was everything to me. Songs clearly expressed my emotions. My dream was to become a singer. *That's not a real job*! *Have you seen any Asian singers in France?* One night, buried under my covers, I heard a man's honeyed voice sing these words:

> *J'sais pas son nom*
> *Je n'sais rien d'lui*
> *Il m'a aimé toute la nuit.*[1]

---

1 Serge Gainsbourg, vocalist, 'Mon légionnaire', by Raymond Asso (lyrics) and Marguerite Monnot (music), 1988.

> Don't know his name
> Or anything about him
> He loved me all night long.

My head spun, my heart almost exploded. That song was like a secret message whispered right into my ear. To tell me that I wasn't alone. That I wasn't crazy. That there was such a thing as love between boys. With his cover of 'Mon légionnaire', Serge Gainsbourg had just kindled a flame. An inferno.

*

The tragic events in Cambodia led to our family being scattered over several continents. While we came to rest in France, my father's surviving siblings ended up in the United States— California, to be exact. We spent summer vacations at my uncle's house with him, his wife, and their ten children: six boys and four girls, all much older than I was. To me, my cousins were the epitome of cool. They played basketball, held cookouts at the beach, had girlfriends, and stirred feelings in me to which I could not put a name.

The ethnic backgrounds of their romantic liaisons were a hot topic. I delighted in following the episodes of these family dramas from one summer to the next. Like my parents, my aunt and uncle had a preference for partners of Chinese descent. Much to their chagrin, most of their children coupled up with significant others from Vietnam! The Vietnamese were hereditary enemies. Many Chinese and Cambodian people shared this hatred for historical reasons of rivalries and invasions. You could move among *youn*,[2] do business with them, but intermarry? My uncle's youngest daughter caused a scandal by dating a Korean. We might've hated the Viets, but at least we had a few cultural traits in common with them; we knew how to beat them up. Koreans were something else. They were from another planet! We knew so little about them, not even enough to badmouth them (that same girl cousin had also been secretly seeing an African American. If that had gotten out, she'd have been disowned for life!). All my cousins had, without exception, taken spouses of the opposite sex and Asian descent. Only my older sister, who lived with them, had married a white man, thus becoming the black sheep of the family. Through these stories, I discovered the colour line that fractured romantic relationships, the taboos and hierarchies deep within my family across the sea.

---

2 Khmer ethnic slur for the Vietnamese.

2

My uncle's house was often lively, bustling. One night, as we were sharing a quiet moment in the living room, one of my cousins' friends asked me: *Are you gay?* I didn't understand the question. The issue wasn't one of language, but of vocabulary: my cousins and I didn't speak the same dialect of Chinese and could only communicate in English. I answered the question I'd understood him to be asking: *Yes, I am happy!* Everyone burst out laughing. *So you are gay*, he said, pressing the point. Horrified, my cousin cut him off: *Don't say that!* I don't know what had made his friend say what he did. Were there telltale signs? Gestures, a way of carrying myself that betrayed what I already was, unbeknownst to myself? I didn't know the term *gay* yet, but I could tell it was supposed to define me and carried negative implications. I had to watch my step, stick to the shadows. Attract as little attention and suspicion as possible. Stop providing a target for jeers and gibes. Of course, I could never quite manage it.

The insults would always pop up at the most unexpected moments. A boy at school: *Quit being such a gaywad!* A girl in chorus: *Faggots are gross!* A language teacher during class: *No homos here!* A passer-by: *Fuckin' fairy!* The dominant, legitimate group can ridicule, insult. Its members can shout out, loud and clear, without shame or repercussion, their hatred of others. They don't give a damn about laws or morality. Public spaces are theirs. They know that no one will dare do a thing except laugh even louder. Least of all their targets. For although fear is among the motivators of their aversion, the kind of fear that puts a leaden feeling in your stomach? That's ours. Shame, too. For many of us, this mixture of fear and shame becomes a kind of second skin. Fear and shame may go dormant, but they are revived by insults, which are always near at hand. In his brilliant memoir *Returning to Reims*, Didier Eribon writes:

> To use an insult is to cite the past. [...] Yet, for those at whom it is aimed, it also represents a projection into the future: the dreadful presentiment that such words, and the violence they carry, will accompany you for the rest of your days.[3]

*

In the early 1990s, the Canal+ TV network aired *My Own Private Idaho*. I was hypnotized by its raw, cruel images, especially the sex scenes. The story of that community of boys who rented their bodies out to other men turned my world upside down. Among them were Mike, an epileptic junkie played by the alluring River Phoenix, and Scott, a rebellious heir brought to life by the dazzling Keanu

---

3 Didier Eribon, *Returning to Reims* (Michael Lucey trans.) (Los Angeles: Semiotext(e), 2013), p. 198.

Reeves. I identified with Mike's character: prickly, oversensitive, a mad dog. Like him, I was hopelessly in love with a boy I thought of as my best friend, a middle-school classmate of mixed race, half French and half Algerian—handsome, popular, charismatic. The total opposite of myself—diffident, withdrawn, unconfident, uncomfortable in my own skin. I couldn't understand why he even hung out with me. Aware of his charms, he was already notching up the girls on his belt. I did not dare open myself up to him.

In a towering, terrifying scene from the movie, the two main characters wind up in the woods, where they make a campfire. Mike asks his companion in misfortune how he feels about him. Scott replies that he only sleeps with men for money, and that two people of the same sex can never really love each other. The junkie disagrees, confessing his love for his 'good friend'. Scott beckons him over and holds him, comforting him. I was dumbfounded. For one, because Mike had managed to speak of his love in so many words. For another, because Scott, although unable to accept Mike's feelings, did not reject him either. I cherished the idea that such a scene would play out the same way between me and my best friend: 'I love you,' I'd say; he'd open his arms and I would press myself against him.

Not long after, two other films became my gay landmarks: Cyril Collard's *Savage Nights*, which depicted a bisexual, HIV-positive protagonist anchoring a destructive love triangle, and Jonathan Demme's *Philadelphia*, the story of a lawyer with AIDS who sues his firm for wrongful dismissal. In these films, as in the media and the public conversation at the time, homosexuality was constantly associated with AIDS, disease, and death. The 'AIDS cocktail', or combination antiretroviral therapy, had yet to make its debut, and the virus was still tearing through homosexual communities. When it first reared its head in the early 1980s, the virus was called 'gay cancer'. Far-right-wing politician Jean-Marie Le Pen went so far as to say: *People with AIDS are like lepers.*[4] It was how I imagined my life would look: exposed to stigma and mortal danger. Was a life like that even worth living?

---

4 On the weekly French political show *L'heure de vérité* [The hour of truth, 1982–1995], 6 May 1987, broadcast on Antenne 2.

3

In high school, boys went out with girls, girls went out with boys, and I didn't score with anyone. I sat out the game in the closet, not a single uncloseted person in sight. My best friend was my best friend no more. He'd found a new group, the 'cool' kids. When I'd approach him in the school courtyard, the jeers would ring out: *Here comes your boyfriend*! Mutual embarrassment. First we stopped hanging out in public, and then we stopped hanging out altogether. Between classes, it was just me and my portable CD player. I didn't draw much attention, and most of the time, people left me to my own devices.

I felt terribly lonely and tried to meet other gay people my age, to make friends. When I found out there was such a thing as the Paris Gay and Lesbian Centre,[5] I sought it out in the 11th arrondissement and stumbled into a session for young people. Everyone was sharing their distress, their loneliness, their trauma. Horrific stories about suicidal teens kicked out of their own homes, already ravaged by life. It was a place to pour your heart out and be

---

[5] Founded in Paris in 1993 to address the ongoing AIDS crisis, this organization is now known as Centre LGBTQI+ de Paris et d'Île-de-France and focuses on countering homophobia in French society.

comforted. We all found a new family there, brought together by suffering. We all gave off the same angst and unease. Their distress was mine, but I couldn't stand hearing about it, watching this group-cry session. Suddenly, I who had always longed to be listened to didn't have a thing to say. Or at least not like this. I had to get out of there as fast as I could, or come my turn, I'd wind up opening the floodgates and drown.

I distanced myself from that atmosphere, trying to meet boys in other ways. I discovered all sorts of ads in a free gay magazine: personals, party phone lines, listservs on Minitel, the French ancestor of the World Wide Web. I spent a lot of time on 3615 GPH, a popular gay dating site of the 1990s, and the phone bill skyrocketed. My first username was *friendship*. That's all I was after. But no matter what, it all came back to sex. I'd ghost on people, stand them up. The idea of meeting someone, much less physical contact, was already terrifying, even though the sexual curiosity was definitely there.

I built up a conversation with a polite man who inspired trust. He was a lawyer, he said, in his 30s and living alone. With a mixture of apprehension and excitement, I went over to his place, a fancy apartment in the 16th arrondissement. I must have been fifteen or sixteen. When he opened the door, my enthusiasm plummeted and fear took over again. The man had light chestnut-brown hair and looked fairly unremarkable—neither handsome nor repulsive. We went to the living room, sat down on the sofa, and he immediately began to undress. It was all going too fast. He asked me to lick his chest. I remained frozen. He insisted. I said I had to go. He took my head and pulled it towards his chest. Reluctantly, I did as I was told. Next, he ordered me to lick his armpits. I moved my face under his arm but, nauseated by the smell, could not force out my tongue. *Keep going*, he threatened, *or I'll call your home and tell your parents everything*! At that moment, I saw red. I leapt up, furious, ready to come to blows if need be, and spat out, *Go ahead*! *And I'll call the cops on you for abducting a minor*! He let me leave. I tore down the stairs and was soon outside, panting.

That time, I said no, but there were other times when I found myself unable to react. Faced with a man who looked nothing like he'd claimed, or the photo on his profile. A hand clutching my buttocks or my prick in a cruising zone. A partner who took off his condom without letting me know. More than once, I told myself it wasn't that serious: bad luck, a bad lay, grit your teeth and bear it. For me, brutality, coercion, and risk were inherent to being gay. I'd explain it away, find excuses, keep lowering the bar for acceptability. And then be overcome with remorse. *Why hadn't I left*? *Why didn't I stop*? Until I no longer saw it as a problem. The culture of sex— one might even say rape—among gays deserves interrogation. This penchant for forcing yourself on others. After all, when two men are involved, the balance of power must be equal, consent a given. Because men love sex—anytime, with anyone. Because men know how to say no. So there's no such thing as rape between men. *If you really didn't want to, you could've punched me. That means you wanted it, didn't you, you whore*? Predators, we see others as pieces of meat and run roughshod over their intimacy. Too bad for the younger and more vulnerable who are initiated into sexuality in this way, who take in these behaviours and imagine that this is what sex between men is like.

Once back home, I began pacing. Usually, my parents would get in late from the garment workshop they managed. I was going around in circles, my gaze riveted to the landline, my head racing through various scenarios: what if he called and my parents picked up? What would he tell them? And what would they say? Maybe if I stayed right by the phone, I could intercept the call? Or even better—I could disconnect the line! My threat had just been a bluff. I wasn't seriously thinking of going to the police. I'd gone over to his place, so it was all *my* fault. I'd been asking for it, and now I'd have to pay the price . . . No! I couldn't let it happen! I couldn't let him win! I refused to be at his mercy, to live with something hanging over my head. I'd beat him to it, neutralize his capacity for harm. I was determined to tell my parents everything, whether he called or not. In the end, it could be a blessing in disguise. I was about to unburden myself at last. Come out of the closet. Find refuge with my parents. I'd convinced myself it would all unfold just like in an American show, with those loving, open-minded white families I saw on TV. My parents would take me in their arms and say, *We love you, no matter what.* They came home. I waited until dinner was over, then went to their bedroom and asked to speak with them. My heart was beating fit to burst. *Papa, Mama, I have something to tell you . . . I like boys.* My father left the room. For several months, he refused to speak to me. My mother declared, *We'll take you to see the doctor, he'll cure you.* Clearly, this was no loving white family. But how did things really go down with those loving White families, anyway?

4

The man never called. My parents didn't take me to the doctor either. Instead, they made do with putting on the squeeze—that is, not letting me make calls or go out. But since they were never around, they couldn't very well do much enforcing. Rebel that I was, I'd sneak out, thumbing my nose at their new rules. This, despite the disaster of that inaugural encounter. That was how I made my first forays into the gay bars of Paris's Marais district.

Among those big, ripped guys clad in the latest tight-fitting tees, shaking their hips to the techno beat, I was out of place: a neurotic suburban kid, a skinny teenager adrift in outsized clothes, hiding behind thick glasses, hugging the walls, completely invisible. But my fashion sense wasn't the only thing to blame. No matter how I met people— whether in bars or by Minitel, then in its final days—there was one refrain I'd hear over and over again: *Sorry, not into Asians*. In the eyes of those I met, that was all I was: *Asian*. And apparently, on the ladder of desirability, that was the bottom rung [. . .]. Under the pretext of 'personal taste', everyone felt free to let loose with their racist commentary: *You all look the same, you're all bottoms, you have tiny dicks.*[6]

'Personal taste' is the get-out-of-jail-free card, the branch clung to through thick and thin. It legitimizes every stance, deflects every accusation. The 'personal taste' defence enables people to refute the racist nature of their rejection. Many in France simply see racism as 'an ideology founded on the belief in a racial hierarchy among human groups', as the popular Larousse dictionary puts it. Only a small fraction of the population subscribes to this kind of biological racism; far be it from most French people to think such thoughts.[7] Where love is concerned, the dismissal of an entire group on the basis of ethnicity is called something else: a matter of 'taste'.

Some go so far as to claim they aren't racist because they've slept with 'Black people' before. First come the 'Black friend' card, then the 'Black lover'. They fornicate as if on safari, for the unusual and exotic experience, before scurrying back to the warmth and safety of their own kind. There could well be a tendency for people of the same group to prefer one another. It's only natural to turn towards what is known. Conversely, others may feel attracted to what is least like them and seek partners beyond their own

---

6 Jean-Baptiste Phou, 'La couleur du désir' [The colour of desire], 12 November 2020: https://bit.ly/3ObY9Yq (all weblinks last accessed on 12 July 2023).

7 Nathalie Birchem, 'Le racisme en France: condamné par l'opinion, et pourtant répandu' [Racism in France: Condemned by public opinion, yet widespread], *La Croix*, 18 June 2020: https://bit.ly/469XHAG. This is a news story on the annual report from France's National Advisory Committee on Human Rights (la Commission nationale consultative des droits de l'homme) in the popular Catholic daily.

communities. These two phenomena have always existed, every-where. They don't necessarily indicate hatred of the other or your own kind. The problem arises when such propensities are rooted in or resort to racial prejudices.

Nor is rejection based on ethnic criteria the prerogative of the dominant group or the majority. What plays out in the context of sexual encounters isn't just about power, since populations that are discriminated against can exclude other such populations. So it is that Black people can dismiss Asians, who could do the same to Arabs, who do the same to other Blacks, and so on and so forth, each enlisting stereotypes attributed to other groups. It would be naive to think that minorities are more tolerant across the board merely because they themselves are stigmatized. And if we consider the second definition for 'racism' proffered by Larousse, an 'attitude of hostility systematically directed towards a racially determined category of persons', eliminating an entire ethnicity from the romantic sphere can only be described as racism, no matter the perpetrator. But having reasonable discussions about such matters can be tricky.

For one thing, the moral condemnation of racism has made quite a spectre of it. We forgive a great deal in ourselves to avoid, at all costs, the taint of this label. Such behaviour is very common among homosexuals, some of whom go even farther by proudly protesting: *But I can't be racist! I'm gay!* Another bit of misdirection to escape being lumped in under that demonized description. Being discriminated against in no way immunizes you from becoming an oppressor in turn. And if people from ethnic minorities are guilty of discrimination, the same goes for gays. Without noticing, we can all have racist thoughts and exhibit racist tendencies while stopping short of outright racism. A fearless moral inventory requires lifting the lid and probing these depictions and representations, admitting we are or could have been guilty of such acts.

For another thing, we live in France, a society that claims not to see colour. This belief stems from our pact as a republic to 'ensure the equality of all citizens before the law, without distinction for origin, race, or religion'.[8] France would have its values be universal, their mission applicable beyond a merely institutional framework. Thus some people are able to convince themselves that such values carry over into their own vision of the world, including the romantic sphere. Like a Frenchwoman I knew who'd been living in Cambodia for a long time. One evening at a gathering, she told me: *I don't see colour, I only see human beings.* And yet she'd never had a partner who wasn't White, de facto excluding all Others. How strange it is to assert, on the one hand, that you don't see differences, and on the other, to base preferences on those very differences. Clearly you see *something*—but what, exactly? To get around the word 'race', a taboo word in France, we resort to other terms that suit our fancy: ethnicity, origin, ancestry ... but it doesn't matter. The results are the same. Boasting of not seeing difference while engaging in discrimination is at best denial, at worst hypocrisy.

Turn me down because I'm not to your taste—I can take that. But that wasn't what I was hearing. I was being rebuffed solely because I was of Asian descent, so consistently that it was becoming

---

8 Article 1 of the Constitution of France, adopted on 4 October 1958.

a pattern. This wasn't about individual tastes expressed by just a handful of people, but in fact a widespread attitude, a kind of conditioning with collective roots. So I began to wonder. Why were Asian males so undesirable? Was there something intrinsically unsightly about us? Were our bodies, our skin, our features fundamentally repulsive? Grotesque!? You can't claim an entire people are unattractive by nature. There must be some other reason, having to do with the perception of the people in question. While Asians weren't inherently repulsive, they did suffer from constructed representations. No one is *born* undesirable, they *become* it.

In the West, the image of the feminized or desexualized Asian male is partly inherited from the colonial era, when native men were reified. They were made to seem less virile or even less human in order to discredit them with women both native and White (read: *pure*), the latter of whom had to be protected from impure admixture. Later, male colonizers allowed themselves homosexual experiences with their serving boys. The same pattern repeated itself wherever Western countries expanded their conquests, varying according to the people being colonized. If Asian men were considered asexual labourers, Black men were seen as hypersexualized beasts that had to be tamed, while Arab men were deemed conquerors and dominators. In every instance, natives constituted the White man's workforce, their domination justified by racialized theories. As early as the nineteenth century, Orientalist and scholar Ernest Renan wrote:

> Nature has made a race of laborers: it is the Chinese race,
> with its marvelous manual dexterity and hardly any feeling

of honor [...] The Negro is a race of field laborers [...]
The European race is a race of lords and soldiers [...] Let
all do what they are made for, and everything will go well. [9]

Thus the figure of the Chinese man as a menial, meticulous
hireling—in short, a machine—was already at work. This archetype,
which continued to propagate over the centuries, would inform
popular culture and be applied to all Asian peoples. Even now, it's
common on the continent to refer to anyone from Asia as 'Chinese'.
So it is that in the collective imagination of the West, the Asian
man remains associated with a nimble, docile workforce. Despite
their presence in France dating back to before the First World War,
Asians are rarely represented in film and media in the country. And
when they are, the depictions are caricatures, or demeaning: most
often a geek, a waiter, or a martial arts expert (this last the only area
in which Chinese men are permitted a semblance of virility). The
Asian man is never the romantic lead, has no emotional or sexual
life. He is, in short, sexless. This conviction infiltrated my mind at
a very early age. In a scene from the 1995 movie *Beyond Rangoon*,
the protagonist, played by Patricia Arquette, is about to be raped
by a Burmese soldier. When I saw that as a teen, instead of focusing
on the tragic violence, I thought: *She won't feel a thing*! Without
realizing it, I'd already internalized the myth of the small penis.

---

9 Ernest Renan, 'Intellectual and Moral Reform of France' [1871] in *'What Is a
Nation?' and Other Political Writings* (M. F. N. Giglioli ed. and trans.) (New York:
Columbia University Press, 2018), p. 232.

5

In the gay world, Asian men are also seen as poorly endowed, effeminate, frail, hairless, passive, and as a result, excluded from the meat market of fuckable men. Save for a handful of men who are aficionados, fascinated by those smooth, firm, slender bodies. The Asian man's body is thus exoticized and eroticized. Men who love *only* Asians have their own special places to go.

I tried my luck at such a place. I went to an evening hosted by the Long Yang Club,[10] and was spotted right away. Men hurled themselves at me like a horde of sharks at fresh meat, utterly without restraint. I was felt up to the tune of *I'll gobble you up raw, my little shrimp!* and *How much do you charge?*

They weren't seeing me. They were trying to match me with the image they had in their heads and would put me back in my place: *You should shave! Facial hair looks ugly on Asians.*

By dint of being pigeonholed, labelled and catalogued, I wound up doing the same.

---

10 The Long Yang Club was founded in the mid 1980s as a social club for gay Asian and Westerners to integrate at a variety of social events within London. The Paris chapter of this association, established in 1993, was the first in France.

ASIAPHILE. *noun.* Synonyms: *Asian Persuasion, Rice Queen*

Definition: an Asiaphile is (often but not always) a White man who loves people of Asian descent. He's on the lookout for the scented pleasures and inscrutabilities of Asia, as made flesh in ephebes with smooth, svelte bodies. But it doesn't just stop at sexual attraction. It's also a love of the Oriental climes where he spends his every vacation. A certified expert in Asian cultures, he waxes explanatory on the history, geopolitics, manners, and customs of all the lands where he's sojourned, and even a few where he's never set foot. To impress you, he'll utter a few words of Thai, Bahasa, or Sinhala. He is also capable of ethnically profiling at a single glance, guessing the nationality of every Asian who crosses his path. Getting it wrong never offends him; he'll just try his luck with the next man. Physically, he's rather run-of-the-mill, not very sure of himself most of the time, often conflicted about his own masculinity, and in great need of reassurance, falling back on boys who look less virile to him and might bolster his ego. In terms of sexual role, he is a top, though not regularly so. He might come off as liking to be in control, but behind closed doors, he'd rather be kept on a tight leash. Sometimes mocked for his extravagant taste, he is convinced he's discovered a treasure trove, and that others know nothing of what truly matters in life.

Game over. I didn't feel like playing any more.

Was this what my romantic life boiled down to? Being considered solely through a racial lens? Moreover, why did people insist on classifying me as *Asian*? What did any of us have to do with each other? I'd never felt I had anything in common with someone from Japan or Indonesia, much less Mongolia. Why was I constantly being defined with reference to my so-called roots? That part of the world was entirely foreign to me. I'd never set foot there, knew nothing of its history, which wasn't my own. I was French. Lay off with all that Made-in-China crap!

I realized that I had to live in a world that didn't want me. A hetero world that didn't want me. A gay scene that didn't want me. Although I was only a teenager, I already faced a pivotal choice: conform, fight back, or give up.

6

I refused to give up on my love life before it had even begun. There must be other options besides the toxic gay scene or ravenous Asiaphiles. Above all, I had to protect myself. Never again did I go to the Marais or events organized by the Asian Lovers. I sought out spaces where I could exist without exposure to constant hostility. So it was that I came to discover get-togethers for Afro-Caribbeans, the Algerian folk music known as raï, and the classic French *bal musette*, or accordion dances: sub-subcultures deep within the gay subculture. A certain goodwill presided at these gatherings. By the same token, I no longer frequented those who constantly rejected me: White people. For me, they became personae non grata. It wasn't merely pre-emptive discrimination, but also an activist gesture. In this way, refusing to sleep with them itself became a form of protest. I wanted those I deemed oppressors to know that where my body was concerned, ¡*No pasarán*!

How radical my positions were is up to debate, the logic and foundation of my approach open to question. Some might even condemn what could be described as 'anti-White racism' (a term little used at the time) on my part. You can't fight exclusion with exclusion, they'd say. Just ignore people who ignore you; don't make a big deal out of it. It's pointless and counterproductive, since to them, you don't even exist. By acting as you do, you only hurt yourself. These same people would round it all off by claiming the only power our oppressors have over us is the power we give them. But tell all that to a teenager getting slapped in the face with 'No Asians' all day long, a teen who, by dint of constantly seeing red, wound up seeing the world only in black and white.

Besides, it wasn't as if turning my back on White people made me suddenly interested in everyone else. Sure, like any '90s teen, I'd grown up with the very Hollywoodian image of heroes embodied by Richard Gere, Patrick Swayze, and Kevin Costner. Always the same pale-looking lead popping up at every turn in shows and music. But I was just as aroused by a whole bunch of other men I was seeing on film: Tony Leung, Will Smith, Gael Garcia Bernal, to name but a few. I gulped down MTV music videos, joyfully fantasizing about 2Pac (for me, the video for 'Temptations' epitomized eroticism), D'Angelo, Usher, and other singers from the R&B and hip-hop scenes who gave off highly sexualized images of themselves. And my immediate, extremely multi-ethnic environment offered a broad palette of boys who thrilled me to my core, like Malagasy and Sri Lankan classmates, or my older brother's mostly Caribbean and Arab friends. Deep within each group, each individual, I discerned special features and unique charms. I decided then and there that my quest would be about these beauties, and that even a lifetime wouldn't suffice to explore them all.

So it was that at the age of sixteen, I met my first boyfriend, a Guadeloupean a dozen years older than me. I was still a high school junior, and he was already cobbling together a living from jobs whose nature I didn't really understand. He lived in a studio in the northwestern suburb of Asnières, and I'd regularly take the bus-RER-C-Metro-commuter-train combo to see him. Now and then, he'd come pick me up in a car. Stylish sedans, never the same one twice, since one of his gigs was penning reviews for an automotive magazine. To me, this was the height of class. My boyfriend swinging by school or home in a sweet ride. To my great chagrin, I had no one to brag about it to; we'd see each other in secret, and I took countless precautions, made up countless excuses to be with him. He introduced me to sexual pleasure. I couldn't have dreamed of a better *first*. A man I was madly in love with, who proved attentive, patient, reassuring. Perfect. We could never get enough of each other's bodies. Ours was a devouring passion. I loved him intensely, as only a teen could, as you love your first love.

A few months before the baccalaureate put an end to high school, I felt myself sprouting wings. The year was 1998. The French football team had just won the World Cup. The entire country was ecstatic. I was ready, confident. I came out to a classmate. A few days later, a female friend told me there were rumours going around about me. I was being called a *fucking faggot*, and soon I'd have a target on my back. At home, the situation with my parents hadn't gotten any better and was maybe even worse. The noose was tightening. I had to flee this increasingly hostile environment, leave before I was caught or thrown out. But I wasn't alone any more. I was invincible. When I turned seventeen, I vanished into thin air. I quit school and joined my boyfriend in his new venture. Not long after, we left for Martinique to live together and build his business—he and I and a few others.

But once there, there was no ti' punch under the coconut palms or close dancing to zouk music. I found myself shanghaied into a sordid pyramid scheme that might as well have been a sect, working like mad, trying to offload cosmetics and dietary supplements to pedestrians in the street, grow my network of resellers for revenues that never topped a hundred-odd euros, living off bread or ramen, reduced to skin and bones, that skin covered in suppurating eczema, with no money to rent a room and no one to put me up, bouncing from sofa to sofa, then in abandoned houses, then on the streets, eating out of dumpsters.

All this because I'd been suckered by the promise of fortune and a place in the sun with my new family. *The only thing standing between you and wealth is your mental attitude. Dig hard and long enough, and you'll strike gold.* My head had been stuffed full of such ideas. I'd even get woken up in the middle of the night for brainwashing, indoctrination sessions that went on for hours. But once I found the strength to fight back, to break free of the organization and the man who'd conned me into it, dug up a job washing dishes at a restaurant to earn my daily bread—and I mean that literally—then I became an enemy, a pariah. I was renounced, attacked, ostracized. And so, at the age of nineteen, I found myself alone, annihilated, far from everything I knew.

No one wants to be a victim. The mere word evokes weakness, helplessness. So we tell ourselves a different story. All we did, we did for love; it was a choice. All this was but a test. To prove that we were strong. That we could take it. And yet it must be said: we were in another man's thrall. Because he paid attention to us, because he said *I love you*, because he made us come. It must be said that he took advantage of our youth, our naiveté, our self-hatred. We had to admit to ourselves that we were victims. And that even if it didn't kill us, it left indelible marks, invisible scars with which we would now have to learn to live.

II

1

I went back to my parents, who'd moved in the meantime. Their business had gone belly-up, and they'd gone from a house in the nice suburbs to a low-income housing project in the deprived *banlieue*. They asked no questions about my protracted absence, and I volunteered no answers. Instead, we chose silence, as we so often did in my family. They were relieved to see me again, and I was relieved to have room and board. I wanted to leave everything I'd gone through behind me, to become human again. As I had few skills and no degree, I picked up odd jobs and kept a low profile. Until it took hold of me again: the desire to meet men. It was the early 2000s, the millennium when all things were possible.

Internet sites had supplanted other ways of hooking up. A world without boundaries, a vast candy store open 24/7 worldwide! But not for me. The rejection I once met with had migrated online in a recurring, systematic fashion. The very common *No Asians, no femmes* posted on profiles everywhere echoed in my ears like the infamous British sign in Shanghai's Huangpu Park: *No dogs, no Chinamen.* When I wasn't ignored, I was sometimes treated to racist insults. *Beat it, chink. Slant-eye. Ching chong.*

On the other side of the screen, people played innocent. *I can fuck whomever I want!* No one claimed to be policing sex. Dictating who could sleep with whom. It wasn't about forcing an accounting of what was beyond dispute, but rather calling into question the way tastes were hierarchized. Wondering why some categories were dismissed out of hand, and so violently. For not everyone was subject to the same treatment.

Prejudices targeting men from other minorities seemed to make them more attractive. Black people were seen as stallions nature had generously endowed, Arabs as alpha males. Only Whites enjoyed the freedom to define themselves, to showcase traits or personal tastes. In the ultra-liberal marketplace of dating sites, every delicacy was on offer: twinks, daddies, bears, underwear, leather, S&M . . . Ethnicity was just one more flavour among many, Asians the lowest rung in the food chain. Like femmes, fats, and olders, they deserved only to live off others' leavings. Such was the fate of those who did not live up to the standards of hairy, muscular, well-hung manliness.[1]

Penis size is an obsession among gays. It was common in profiles to describe yourself in terms of this (*BM* for *bien monté* or 'well hung', *TBM* for 'very well hung'), to list it as a feature you were seeking, or to demonstrate exclusivity (*TBM* seeks *TBM* was just as common). Pleasure derived solely from penis calibre. Kitted out with the necessary tools—ruler and tape measure—you had to provide precise measurements for your artillery: length and girth.

---

1 Phou, 'La couleur du désir'.

People took care to send pics from every angle, requiring others to do the same. False advertising was off-limits when it came to the merchandise!

Gays inherited the sexist and misogynistic values of heteronormative society, making them their own, escalating them: the alpha male was put on a pedestal, an object of desire. Fags were fine, but not fairies. In a *Slate* article 'But why do gay men have such muscular bodies?' sociologist Sylvain Ferez explains the origin of this body worship:

> This image became prevalent in the post-AIDS era. The idea was to show fit, aesthetically pleasing bodies to counter the image of the sickly, ill-fated gay man. It was adopted, and now we have an excessively powerful normative pressure.[2]

This stigma needed reversing: from effeminate (femme) or diseased (poz) gays to muscular, attractive gays. In addition to these physical qualities, the new gay was also cultured, well off, refined. In the media and in new social circles, gays became a cultural endorsement: the hip, quirky, party-loving friend. Later on, a classmate told me: *I love gay men! You guys really know how to light up a party!* How disappointed she was when I confessed I was more of a homebody! She'd thought she was paying me a compliment, that she'd found a wingman for her night-time pursuits. She covered

---

2 Fabien Jannic-Cherbonnel, 'Mais pourquoi les gays ont-ils des corps si musclés?' [But why do gays have such muscular bodies?], *Slate*, 6 August 2016: https://bit.ly/3PMAVcu.

for herself as best she knew how: *Oh, you must get that from your Asian side!*

The gay man even embodies the ideal consumer, of enhanced purchasing power, whose wallet must be targeted. In short, he possesses every quality, and now it's OK to be his friend. But don't push it—there's a still a long way to go before we're OK with them being our children. In the same piece, Ferez comments on the uniformity of gays' representation in the media: 'These images are also the result of a French system that seeks a single legitimate representation. Society finds a homogenous homosexual group very reassuring.'

These categories enable us to tell the difference between who *is* and who *isn't*. Because we need to be able to tell. Make a distinction between *them* and *us*. It is a way of refusing to accept that gay people can be found in every social class, every profession, every ethnicity, every age, every scene, every territory, every kind of family. In Cambodia, a female friend once said to me in utter seriousness: *I can't pick them out any more. When I see a gay couple, I can't even tell which one's the woman.* But really, nothing had changed. It was simply that before, she'd *thought* she could tell who was sleeping with whom, and how.

Gays have gotten used to this image because it offers up a new-found respectability. We've gone from being less than human to superhuman. To drive away shame and scorn, we no longer simply proclaim our pride in ourselves. We have other reasons to be proud, for we are *better* than heteros. When it comes to calling yourself gay, loving men and sleeping with them won't cut it any more.

We must be the incarnation of a superman who in his superiority will naturally be White, of course. So no femmes! No Asians! No fats! No olders! No pozzes! No uglies! No Blacks! No Arabs! No poor people! No cripples! No transvestites! No transsexuals! No bridge-and-tunnel! No hicks! We don't want them in our beds, or out of them. People like that don't deserve to be welcomed into our rainbow nation of the hot and the ripped, much less to represent it, whether on TV or in magazines. People like that should be shunted off to the sidelines, out of view. Hide the gays I don't want to see. After being hated for so long, we want to revel in the flattering image others have of us now, the flattering image we have of ourselves.

All this is but a delusion. No stigma ever really gets reversed. All we do is create smokescreens and new, equally destructive chimeras. And making yourself a group's gay mascot only lasts a little while. True colours always end up showing, and hate is never far away. We're brought back to cold reality when hundreds of thousands of demonstrators pour into the streets, rising up against gay marriage, chanting that a family is a daddy, a mommy, and kids; when statistics attest to a steep rise in violence towards us, not to mention parents who kick their children out of their own home, psychos who toss them off rooftops, homophobically driven ambushes and murders. The hardest part, on either side, will be seeing a gay man as no more or less than a human being. Without innate qualities or intrinsic vices. Will be admitting that as a group, homosexuals too are subject to collective mechanisms, with our solidarities and our oppressions. That we are human beings, with all the best and worst that human beings have to offer.

2

Thanks to my command of English, I found a job as a temp at an Air France call centre. I met some amazing people there, among them a French-Moroccan woman who spoke French, Arabic, German, English, and Spanish fluently. She'd picked up all these languages from her family background and time spent abroad, except for Spanish, which she claimed to have learned from books. Fascinated, I set myself the challenge of doing the same. I dove daily into language textbooks and joined dating sites in Spain to acquire a more specialized vocabulary. One day, I was chatting with a Paris-based Colombian on vacation in Madrid. When he got back to Paris, we decided to get to know each other better and ended up becoming friends. He introduced me to a fellow countryman interested in a language exchange. It was love at first sight.

This *paisa* from the northwestern coffee-growing region of Antioquia worked in construction with his brother, lived with his female cousin, and spent all his time in an exclusively Spanish-speaking environment. As his immigration status was uncertain, he didn't like to show his face in public, and didn't get much chance to speak French. Still, I confess to having gotten more out of our exchanges than he did. We only ever spoke in Spanish. He introduced me to several aspects of Latin American and Spanish culture in the original: the literature of Gabriel Garcia Marquez, Isabel Allende, and Mario Vargas Llosa, the cinema of Pedro Almodóvar, Julio Medem, and Alejandro Amenábar, even the music of Chavela Vargas, Mercedes Sosa, and Shakira (back when she was a brunette and sang in Spanish).

He had a hectic social life and introduced me to friends from Colombia, Mexico, Ecuador, and even Brazil. I'd never suspected there were so many gay Latin Americans in Paris. Some dated others in their group, but most of them were in relationships with French people, often with the same configuration: an older White man and a Latino living off him or receiving money, clothes, and other gadgets. No one ever mentioned prostitution. Instead, they said: help, support, presents. And in this barter system, everyone flaunted their capital. Economic for Whites, symbolic for Latinos. For among the ethnic categories, they were at the top of the pyramid, even if many of them were pretty far from the image of the tempestuous Latino, brawny and *caliente*. They had the right nationality and the right accent—that was enough. Some played up these charms, laying the romantic 'Latin lover' on thick, doing what they had to in order to be believable, acting jealous without going too far. Most of them juggled lovers and sugar daddies. No one was fooled, everyone found their niche.

Our couple was seen as an exception. We stood apart. His circle considered me one of theirs: he and I were about the same age, I was an unlucky exotic type just like them, and now I spoke their language. I made new friends, and we were often invited to wild parties. After one of these, my boyfriend asked me:

Viste como te miró este chico? Did you see how that guy was looking at you?

Creo que te equivocas. I think you're mistaken.

¿Sabes que la gente te mira? You do know people look at you?

No es verdad. That's not true.

Pues si, la gente te nota. Como te he notado yo. It sure is. People notice you. Just like I noticed you.

Pero ¿por qué? But why?

Porque tienes algo especial. Porque eres guapo. Because there's something special about you. Because you're handsome.

That proved a pivotal moment for me. No one had ever told me such a thing before. No one had ever *seen* me. And because someone now did, I could look at myself differently as well. No longer as someone who was *not bad for a Chinese man, with nice smooth Asian skin*. Just *handsome*: end of story. I could see myself, maybe, as someone unique.

Our affair lasted a few more months; then we decided to go our separate ways. By the time we broke up, he had a grasp of French and I, Spanish. But he had taught me much more. That there were still things out there to be discovered, experienced. That maybe it wasn't all pointless.

3

Most of my coworkers had their temp contracts renewed, but not me. The official reason was a drop in airline activity due to the 9/11 attacks, but if you ask me, it was more about an altercation with a floor manager and the warning that had followed: *You're not like the other Asians. They're respectful and obedient. You talk back!* I preferred to walk out with my head held high and a severance package. I bought a one-way ticket to Madrid for a change of scene, and to polish up my Spanish. Once there, I found a roommate situation and a job in a Spanair call centre. I loved going for long strolls, a *flâneur* in the streets of the Spanish capital, eating in tapas bars, and at long last, enjoying my twenties. It was time to lift my boycott and explore new pleasures: not all White people could be racist oppressors.

The Madrid neighbourhood of Chueca was rife with *musculocas*, men obsessed with getting swole. Their tight outfits and techno music recalled the muscle queens of the Marais. Neither of us was really what the other was looking for. But unlike in France, I encountered far less hostility about my ethnic appearance. Not that there was no racist behaviour at all—when I walked by, I'd often hear people mimicking karate cries or shouting *chinito*—but any move I made didn't meet with automatic rejection, and *No locas, no Asiáticos* wasn't a thing. Rather, I aroused curiosity. Boys would come up to me. I wasn't invisible any more (even if, according to my Colombian, I never had been in the first place). Now I took in their glances, smiled back, and started conversations, which always kicked off the same way: *¿De dónde eres?* The classic *Where are you from?*

In France, this question would annoy me. It was always the first or second thing people asked, a photo finish with *So what do you do for a living?* I was careful to dodge the question and return the courtesy: *And you? Where were you born? How about your parents? And your grandparents? Fancy that! I've never been to Amiens, it must be so exotic! Do you speak Picard, then? Can you cook regional delicacies?* My conversational partners rarely appreciated the gambit. The humour or absurdity went right over their heads, and the talk usually petered out, which suited me just fine. What I wanted was to give off a vibe of *If you bring up my roots, watch out! Ask me about ANYTHING else but THAT!* I'd rather have sanded off my skin, made it see-through, so it wouldn't be a topic of discussion.

When I think back, I was probably hung up about my origins, that part of my history I knew nothing about. I never had much to say, so I preferred to cut things short. Such talk would inevitably lead me back to my parents, their silence, my own ignorance, that part of my identity with nothing attractive about it, in my opinion. This put would-be suitors in an impossible situation. Some of them were no doubt genuinely, wholesomely interested in finding out more about me. Especially since I was happy to ask about the origins of non-White boys I met. But from *Frenchmen of strictly European ancestry,*[3] it felt like an act of aggression. *Where are you from?* meant I wasn't actually French, that my presence in Gallic territory needed justifying.

Things were so different in Spain. Since I wasn't Spanish, it seemed only natural for people to ask the question. When I replied that I was French, the usual queries would follow: *No, but where are you really from? How about your parents? Why don't you have a French accent? What are you doing in Spain?* No matter my answer, I saw the surprise on their faces. Nothing fit with the image these people had of me in their heads. I wasn't like a Frenchman, or your usual Asian. All this amused me a great deal, and I delighted in sowing confusion. I even toyed with it. I no longer experienced my Asianness as a turnoff, but instead a lure I used to my advantage. I milked it for all it was worth, playing whatever Orientalism I needed up to the hilt. I overindulged mandarin collars, so-called ethnic patterns, and acted the sage when I spoke, slowing my gestures. One man even told me: *Pareces muy místico.* Indeed, mystical was exactly how I seemed! I remembered that when I tried my hand at drag and picked a stage name for myself: Mystica.

What I had going for me, above all else, was the bloom of youth, and I knew it. I hurled myself into madly chasing down sex and debauchery. Tall, short, fat, skinny, old, young, hot, ugly, hairy, shaven, brown-haired, blond, ginger . . . I never passed up an opportunity;

---

3 A term borrowed from Léonora Miano, *Afropea* (Paris: Grasset, 2020), forthcoming in English translation by Gila Walker (London: Seagull Books, 2024).

nothing was off limits. It was about the unbridled pursuit of pleasure, a desire for transgression, but also my own rehabilitation in a way, proving to my own eyes that I was attractive, desirable. I also needed to take back my own body, just like Virginie Despentes asserted in *King Kong Theory*: after her rape, sex and prostitution were a way of building herself back up. For me, this sexual frenzy proved salutary. By testing the limits of my body, I was glueing it back together piece by piece. My misadventure in Martinique hadn't been the end of me. There was a part inside that still wanted to live, to experience pleasure.

*

I went back to France and continued to work at call centres. I returned to living with my parents briefly before finding a studio in the southern Paris suburb of Arcueil. My first pad all to myself! I was still hungry for new adventures, new horizons. My meagre income went mostly to travel. I scoured the cities of Europe on a shoestring thanks to budget companies and youth hostels. I always prepared for these trips the same way: the popular French travel series Guide du Routard for the daytime, and the Spartacus Gay Travel Index for the night. By day, I'd hit the tourist sites. When the sun went down, I'd slip into a parallel universe, a kind of secret society with its codes and rituals. Ways of being spotted, making contact, signalling your attraction to someone else, taking up or turning down advances. Finding out about gay life and meeting up with gays in different cities went beyond the merely carnal. There were institutions and venues that provided spaces for socialization and solidarity. I was welcomed as a member of the community, introduced to other people and places off the beaten track. Here I'd be offered a guest room, there initiated into new aspects of gay culture and the culture that called itself mainstream.

In the major European cities, I'd run into all sorts of nationalities and ethnicities. I felt like I'd slipped into the skin of an explorer setting out to meet the people of the world through sex. I racked up the notches on my belt, each new conquest seeming wildly exotic: a Croatian! An Egyptian! A New Zealander! Contrary to my own principles, I began establishing categories, making comparisons. In the same way, some men told me I was their *first Asian*. So I was an ambassador, then! I had to be crushing it all the time, I had to *represent*. I wanted to avenge my race, restore our honour. I gladly took on the role of 'Asian' within the set framework of cold, anonymous, transactional sex, along with everything potentially dehumanizing about it.

Therein lies the exhilarating aspect of such encounters: you never really want to get to know the other person. You deprive them of their individuality and sum them up in a few features: skin colour, nationality, even religion. A bit like with porn: you search for keywords depending on what you're in the mood for at the moment. Whether it's masturbating to an actor or sleeping with an actual person, those people are reduced to images, fantasies. When you treat someone else as an object, you can't protest when they do the same to you. Some even find this highly titillating—I did. It works as long as you play by the rules of the game, which admittedly may not be for everyone. The concern arises when you step outside the framework, when you don't want to be seen as an experiment, or a sexual category. Still, some people unilaterally grant themselves the right to objectify others on the basis of race, especially in virtual hook-up spaces where anonymity reigns. It might be a harmless bit of fun for them, but for the targets of their mockery it can feel especially violent, as ethnic appearance produces effects in other aspects of life as well. You can't keep your skin in the closet the way you hang up latex accessories.

4

I continued my exploration of skins and bodies, never denying myself any kind of pleasure. Instead, it was others who denied me. Indeed, other Asians stubbornly avoided me, resorting to stock phrases I found puzzling. My advances offended them because they weren't actually 'lesbian', because sex between Asians was seen as incestuous, because the promise of pleasure could be fulfilled only by a Caucasian cock. Not to forget the recurring *I don't do communalism*. These excuses are compelling and deserve closer individual scrutiny.

The first reason cited for Asian men not sleeping with each other is sexual incompatibility. Deeply rooted in the gay imagination is the idea that Asians can only be passive, a bottom. And since two bottoms won't do, they need to seek partners outside their ethnic group. Or even that Asians are associated with femininity; rather, effeminacy. In which case the argument goes: I am a woman and I don't sleep with other women. Here, the allusion to lesbians is pejorative, deliberately mocking.

There is no question that Asian men can be passive, effeminate, or transsexual. But can such traits be applied to all of them, or are these merely models imposed by representations that limit the field of the possible? For claiming that all Asians are passive implies they can't satisfy each other. We're back to sacralizing the phallus. And since all Asians have tiny phalluses, they can't possibly make good lovers. Such beliefs have wreaked havoc on our psyche and have repercussions on our actual performance. We convince ourselves of their truth, conferring on them the strength of a self-fulfilling prophecy. Or we can dare to go where others least expect. That's what one of my friends of Cambodian descent did: to escape the cliché of the Asian bottom, he only ever topped. Alas, in seeking to free ourselves from others' perception, we continue to define ourselves in relation to it.

Second excuse: we can only get off with White partners. Though many groups enjoy flattering reputations as far as sexual prowess goes, they're our favourite. We bestow our favours on them alone. They remain the ideal, the benchmark by which all others are measured; they're the ones we must seduce. Someday we might experiment with the others, for the sake of fantasy or transgression. For there is a difference between sex, dating, and a relationship. Different goals, different partners. Dish towels and cloth napkins don't go in the same drawer.

Next up, the allusion to incest, which might seem absurd or ridiculous. Besides, I've never heard people from other groups ever bring this up (though they well might). Among Asians in France, however, be they men, women, homos, or heteros, this line of thinking is very common. They'll say it out loud and greet it with raucous guffaws, even affection. The most indulgent (or naive) might argue that they're just joking. But this analogy is anything

COMING OUT OF MY SKIN

but light-hearted. Bringing up incest is a way of making something irrevocably forbidden. It's instituting a taboo. Incest also suggests that your partner is too close to yourself: you look too much alike. This reinforces the idea that Asians can't be told apart and have no individuality. More even than members of the same family, we're identical clones.

Last but not least, we come to the idea that Asians who hang out with other Asians are somehow being 'communalist'. On the show *Explain It to Us: What's the Deal with Communalism in France?* aired by French-Monegasque radio station RMC, journalist Bérengère Bocquillon enlightens us as to the origins of this concept:

> In France, communalism has a very negative connotation.
> It's a word that cropped up about fifteen or so years ago in
> the political sphere. A pejorative word, because in France,
> for historical reasons, the State has always brought people
> together, created unity. Communalism is thus seen as a
> threat to the Republic.[4]

Hanging out with people from your own ethnic or cultural group is this seen as undermining the only legitimate community, the nation. It is an act of withdrawal. To be a good citizen, one must blend in, be diluted, dissolve. But not with just anyone. Mixed-race couples are approved of and held up as models when one of the partners is White, the colour of normalcy and neutrality. More even than a pledge of integration, it is also a mark of prestige. In fact, we inevitably expect Asians who conform, no matter their

---

4 Bérengère Bocquillon, '*Expliquez-nous*': *Communautarisme, où en est-on en France?*, BFM avec RMC, 18 February 2020: https://bit.ly/3XKeAOJ.

gender, to the reigning standards for social success and/or beauty, to be coupled up with a member of the dominant group. Having internalized this idea myself, when a beautiful and talented French-Cambodian actress informed me that her partner was Vietnamese, I was incredulous: *But she's so gorgeous! She should be with a real Frenchman! What's she doing with an Asian? Something must be wrong* . . . Dating within your group arouses suspicion, even fear. Such couples are awful communalists, dangerous enemies of the Republic. Other minority groups are of next to no interest, since they don't enable any scaling of the social ladder. Worse yet, hanging out with them could get you bumped a few rungs down. To make sure your image matches up with that of the exemplary, well-integrated minority citizen, you must spend time among Whites, be seen on their arm, brandish them like trophies.

For a member of an ethnic minority, the choice of whom to love thus becomes a political act, whether deliberately or in spite of yourself. Ethnicity might not be the deciding factor when it comes to falling in love, but that won't stop onlookers from projecting all kinds of meanings and judgements onto you and your partner. Depending on the colour of their skin, you might be seen as a 'race traitor' or a worthy representative of your own kind, an upstanding French citizen or a perfidious communalist.

And so, to avoid the ordeal of communalism, you must flee your roots, whether real or alleged. Don't hang out with your own kind in public or in private. I too sought to avoid all contact with Asians, from grade school until I was an adult. It was a reflex. Generally, other Asians did the same thing. A quick glance out of the corner of your eye sealed the tacit deal, and the choreography of dodging one another began. It would be shameful to be seen in the company of that 'sub-breed' you no longer wished to be a part of. You even went so far as to renounce your own body. For a long time, my skin horrified me with its pallor, my eyes with their shape, my nose with its flatness, my fingers with their slenderness, my hair with its stiffness . . . All these characteristics I associated with the condition of being Asian provoked repulsion and disgust. I dreamed of letting my skin roast in the sun, getting implants to be hairier, going under the scalpel—anything to stop looking so *yellow*. In a morbid delirium, I'd rather have been *brown*, a more enviable category in my eyes. Others sought to look more like the norm, act more French than the French, whiter than white.

Paradoxically, the practices of skin bleaching and double eyelid surgery began among Asians living in Asia. Asians in France rarely resort to it. It may be that when you're part of a majority, you seek to assert your originality by copying a Western ideal of beauty, adapting it to yourself, whereas when you're part of a minority, you'd rather not do anything to stand out, and any kind of physical alteration only draws notice. So you pick other external ways of conforming, like your way of speaking or dressing, but most of all, you watch whom you hang out with. This is especially true for those of us who grew up in France, so steeped were we in the Republic's myth of integration. For immigrants, the logic runs the other way. Turning to one's community is often preferable, as it provides access to a familiar cultural environment and sometimes even a mutual support network. But where love is concerned, no matter what generation you are, Asian gays display a clear preference for White partners.

All this is beginning to change. It's increasingly common for Asian men to find each other attractive and couple up. This could be driven in part by the rise of a young generation with fewer complexes, rid of a reductive view of themselves and more aware of power issues within relationships. Perhaps nightlife and pop culture even played their part? In Paris, AZN soirées, founded in 2004, were the first dedicated to young Asian gays. These gatherings lent them a hipper image and provided a space where they could meet. In 2006, the magazine *Baby Boy* featured an Asian model on the cover, its headline 'Special Issue: AZIAN New Wave' showing a sexy, glamorous side—previously, a rare sight. It was the first, and to date, the only time a gay magazine had granted the Asian population such attention.

What's more, Asian men can be spotted here and there in movies and TV series that only traffic in hackneyed clichés. To claim on such a basis that their image has been completely reversed in the Western world, that they're now popular and husband material . . . well, let's not exaggerate. Asian women are subjected to the opposite treatment: hypersexualization. Their appearances on the small and big screen alike, most often as prostitutes or femmes fatales give certain menfolk yellow fever—a fascination with such putatively submissive, lascivious creatures of fantasy.

The web and the explosion of streaming platforms have enabled easier access to diverse affirming and alluring representations of Asian characters, notably in films produced in Asia. One might go looking for positive role models there. One might. But just because someone has physical features like our own isn't enough to make us identify with them. The cultural component is just as vital.

In France, there is a painful lack of models who not only look like us but speak the same language and share the same customs. The mainstream media goes on spewing forth more or less the same representations of Asian bodies. In the West, it's well understood that images are a potent weapon in the arsenal of soft power. The feeling of being economically threatened by Far Eastern countries contributes to the perpetuation of such dehumanizing, even demonizing depictions. Maintain a certain otherness to them, no matter what. When all is said and done, little to nothing has changed in the mental and media spaces of mainstream culture. Asian men might have climbed a few rungs, but they're still near the bottom of the ladder.

5

In 2003, at the age of twenty-two, I went back to school, thanks to programmes for continuing adult education. I'd had it with call centres. I set out to complete a two-year state technical degree in international business in a year. In all my years of schooling, I'd never been more than an average, not to say mediocre student, but suddenly I was discovering new intellectual capacities in myself. I had a thirst for learning and found everything exciting, even statistics and cost accounting, despite my continued ignorance of multiplication tables. I graduated at the top of my class, and my professors encouraged me to push on. I was accepted into a Master's programme in Management at the prestigious Université Paris-Dauphine, and fast-tracked to boot! After a year, I faced the same choice. *Another year, another degree! Can't pick a field yet? Just make money, it'll always come in handy!* my financial analysis professor advised. I took his counsel and was selected to specialize in finance at ESCP Europe, one of France's top-rated business schools. Once a disengaged, disruptive student, I, a suburbanite and immigrant son, now found myself among the crème de la crème. No one could figure out how I'd wound up there, and I regularly faced interrogation from my more sceptical classmates. *Where'd you go for prep class? Your foundation degree? Which high school? What'd you get on your baccalaureate? Specialization? What do your parents do?* Once again, people had a hard time placing me. I was a bug in the system.

My whole time in higher ed, I had no time for anything else. I spent all my days, nights, weeks, and weekends studying. The rest of life got put on hold. A few hook-ups here and there, just enough to get me by. When I was feeling horny, a text to a fuckbuddy, a quick hop to a sauna, an internet connection, and usually, it was all taken care of in under an hour (how straight men deal, I have no idea). In my social life, I was more at ease with myself and open about being gay to everyone, even my sisters. And it didn't seem to be much of a problem. Times were changing. Some found it cool; most didn't care. Except my parents. My mother kept asking if I had a girlfriend, hoping I'd marry a Chinese girl. My father kept up the silent treatment.

In 2005, I took off to Madrid to wrap up my advanced professional training prior to starting a job as an assistant analyst with the Corporate and Investment Banking branch of the French bank Société Générale in Barcelona. I wasn't much interested in investment banking, but I was competitive—with my cohort and myself. It was all about who landed the cushiest gig, the most money, the best lifestyle right out of the gate. I wanted revenge, wanted to see how far up the social ladder I could climb. Wanted to prove, despite my chaotic start in life, that I could do just as well if not better than anyone else. In my sociology class on organizational analysis,

I discovered Pierre Bourdieu's concept of social reproduction and saw things in a new light. Once the invisible forces had been laid bare, I felt like I was no longer at their mercy and possessed a semblance of control over my life.

6

I'd only been to Barcelona once before. Like many, I'd been seduced by its international and cultural dimension, its privileged location between mountains and shore. Now I was about to conquer the Catalan capital like Romain Duris in *The Spanish Apartment*. To my great disappointment, what I found was not Madrid's good-natured, spontaneous, and easy-going atmosphere, so dear to my memory. For me, Barcelona was a cold city, pretentious and inaccessible. Despite how big and cosmopolitan it was, I had a hard time meeting people. I couldn't stand the gay neighbourhood of Eixample. There was still the popular barrio of El Raval with its cramped bars, among them La Bata de Boatiné, where I spent most of my weekends. Little by little, I got my bearings.

Also around this time, I became interested in Asia. I went to Cambodia for the first time. Despite everything I'd projected onto it after years of being afraid to visit, the trip turned out to be utterly mundane: neither love at first sight, nor the wrath of the gods. But something inside me awakened. I figured I probably had more exploring to do. I even began to cherish the idea of living in that part of the world. Back in Spain, I began to study kung fu. Sure, that had nothing to do with Cambodia, but directly or indirectly, it got me closer to my roots. The last thing I wanted was to be one of those Asian caricatures who practise martial arts, but I was drawn by the physical discipline and its Eastern philosophy. Actually, jujutsu, Tibetan meditation, or calligraphy would've probably scratched the itch just as fine. My knowledge of Asia was quite limited, and I made do with what was locally available.

Having settled in a bit, I hoped to get into a more serious relationship, and fantasized about meeting a handsome Spaniard. There was a guy in the locker room at kung fu lessons, and sometimes we'd exchange glances. He was tall, charming, with brown hair and brown eyes. He might have been the tempestuous Spaniard I'd been dreaming of! One day, on my way out of my apartment, I ran into him, and we started chatting. Irony of ironies! He was French. We decided to meet up again.

There was something magical, something extraordinary about that simple chat. We hadn't met in a gay establishment, or online. No, it'd happened just like that—at a sport, a hobby, and then later, in the street. This was a privilege that only heteros usually enjoyed, often impossible for people like us, quite literally for fear of being assaulted. When it came to meeting others, we stayed confined to our own spaces. Gays are often accused of communalism, of ghettoizing themselves. But are they ever really given a choice?

For our first date, we'd picked dinner at a Nepalese restaurant in our neighbourhood, Gràcia. The evening went wonderfully in that colourful, stylish setting, amid the soothing music, the aromas of spices and incense. Given to complaint like any good Frenchmen,

we started out by putting down the city neither of us liked—
Barcelona the overhyped, in our eyes. Then the conversation turned
to our shared passion for foreign travel, our budding interest in Asia.
In fact, he was looking for a job there. What a coincidence! The
night went on. We got to know each other. I started getting butter-
flies in my stomach. When the meal was over, I asked him back to
my place. He turned me down, which sent me spinning into doubt
and uncertainty. What was the matter? Didn't he like me?

Before him, sex had been a tool for socializing, a way of getting
to know people. I shook dicks like one would shake hands. Sex was
a reflex, systematic, mechanical. Immediate consummation. I could
skip dinner and go straight to dessert. It was part of the ritual, one
more mandatory step. It made us machines for fucking. I never
even stopped to wonder if, at the moment, I felt desire.

We met up again a few days later. I went charging right in; he
stepped aside. We began a game of cat and mouse. Until our first
kiss. Until we found our way to the bedroom. At no point in time
did it occur to me that he'd simply wanted to *wait*. That sex wasn't
the only way to get to know someone. That holding back could be
part of the game of love. It was about taking your time. Fanning
the flame of desire. Clearly, this boy had surprises in store for me.
Our passion grew, and plans for living in Asia took shape. We each
started looking for a job in our respective fields in that part of the
world: Hong Kong, Shanghai, Kuala Lumpur . . . It was all wide
open. I was the first to get a few bites. We'd only been seeing each
other for a few months when a job offer came in from Singapore,

and we set out to live this new adventure together. At last, the skies were clearing, and I could picture a life flooded with sunshine. I'd earned this, my share of happiness, and I intended to enjoy it to the fullest.

7

I was living the dream: dream job, dream salary, dream lover. Vengeance was mine. Even my parents were thrilled. My name, which had dropped out of family conversations, was now shouted from the rooftops: our son is working for BNP Paribas in Singapore! Change of scene. Immaculate, orderly metropolis where everyone toed the line. It felt weird seeing Asians in every job, every trade, from policeman to TV host to garbageman. All my representations had been turned upside down.

Society there was highly racialized. Official paperwork asked you to specify your ethnic group. I didn't really know what box to check. Southeast Asian, maybe? Or Chinese? Or even Other. I never answered the same way twice, partly for fun and partly as a provocation. My history was equivocal enough that every category pertained. While apartment hunting, I often saw 'No Chinese, No Indians' in ads. I was puzzled. Weren't Chinese people Singapore's ethnic majority? I was informed that this didn't apply to Singaporeans of Chinese descent: what they meant was mainlanders from China. Within the context of discriminatory listings, the label 'Chinese' referred not to ethnicity but nationality. For Indians, on the other hand, it was about ethnicity and nothing but.

No Singaporeans of Indian descent allowed. At work, I caught onto racial hierarchies by watching people enter the skyscraper where my office was located. The doors opened automatically for Whites, Chinese were asked for badges, Malays were doublechecked, and Indians had to present themselves at the front desk. Me, I had the right nationality, but the wrong face. I would get stopped every morning by security even though, with time, they should have come to recognize me. My coworkers also had trouble with my sweet li'l mug: *Oh, so you're Jean-Baptiste? Sorry, wasn't expecting that!*

Homosexuality was illegal, but that didn't keep an active gay scene from existing, especially since it was good for business and the economy. The question of race also came up in gay relations. For example, a mixed couple like our own consisted of a potato queen (someone non-White with a White) and a rice queen (a non-Asian with an Asian partner). These labels, which seemed impossible to escape, bothered me less than the different ways in which we were treated. My partner had a red carpet at his feet, always had the floor, always got the bill. When I wasn't being actively ignored, I was treated like a prostitute.

I'd made equality a point of honour in our relationship, right down to finances. We split rent and the bills, even though my partner had no income. I took this so far as to open a tab for him, updated regularly on an Excel sheet, while he looked for a job. Let no one say either one of us was taking advantage of the other—equality at any price! But it was no use. No matter what we did, no matter who had more in the bank or a higher social standing, race ruled all. As a White man, he was heir to a symbolic heritage that bestowed upon him power and superiority. In terms of racial capital, my balance would always be in the red, and nothing could ever change that. Equality was but a pipe dream.

Everyone I met predicted that our relationship wouldn't last, that someday he'd leave me for somebody new. In their eyes, I'd hit it big, but there was a price: he was so covetable. Why didn't the reverse hold true? Why wasn't he the one lucky to be with me? I didn't think I had anything to fear from all those potato queens hunting White men out there. They couldn't possibly be competition. I was better than that. *We* were better than that.

What was bound to happen happened. He confessed he'd cheated on me with a Singaporean boy. A host of questions gnawed at me. I wasn't good enough for him—was that it? Why an Asian? Had all those vicious gossips been right? Could nothing else be expected? Were we such caricatures of ourselves, so very unoriginal? He got bogged down in contradictory apologies. He felt alone, he had too much time to himself, too much temptation all around. Looking for a job stressed him out. I didn't offer him enough support. He didn't believe in just one partner. Fair enough. A few days later, I slept with one of his friends, a stunning Indian Singaporean who'd been prowling around me. I took care to notify my partner beforehand and tell him everything afterwards. Tie score, centre ball. A childish game. We both emerged even more wounded.

We tried to save our relationship. Reconciliation, peace and quiet, then back to shouting matches, more frequent and more violent. It was all going downhill. Cracks were showing everywhere in the veneer. Work was hell. I hated my job, felt like a cog in some absurd machine that made money out of money without creating anything of value. I cursed Singapore. I saw it as a bland society of spoiled children whose only thought was for malls and food courts. I loathed this seemingly enviable life. This world of bling-bling and work-hard-play-hard was not for me. They rang hollow, these cardboard cut-out surroundings.

As often as possible, I found myself going to Cambodia, my only breath of fresh air. I took all my vacations there, sometimes even for just a weekend, as the flight was only ninety minutes. It kept me going, but also set my mind awhirl. I didn't know who I was any more, or where I lived. Even as the banking sector was hit full force by the subprime crisis of 2008, I was going through crises myself—of love, work, and self. I had to turn it all around. Not die here, where I stood.

On one of my trips to Phnom Penh, I heard some people were putting on a show, a musical, and there would be open auditions. Singing had been a cherished pursuit since childhood, in choirs and groups, always as an amateur. I lacked any professional stage experience; this would be my first time auditioning. I made a separate trip to Cambodia just to do so. After endless weeks of waiting, I received a positive response from the director. I didn't have to think twice. I tendered my resignation forthwith. *Have you gone completely insane? Why didn't you just ask for a sabbatical? Why didn't you wait for a severance package?* One more day, and I was going to implode. So long, dream job, dream salary, dream lover. I left all that behind to step into a brand-new skin in Cambodia, the motherland.

8

I could breathe free again. Car exhaust, open-air landfills—I drew them deep into my lungs. Scarlet sky, nonstop noise, blazing sun. All my senses were alive, alert. I was living a waking dream: acting in an international production. How surreal it felt, to suddenly be among almost sixty actors, some from Broadway! A childhood dream: to sing and be paid for it. In Cambodia! A land I'd hated, fantasized about, and rediscovered. A land not yet fully healed from its civil wars and genocide. Everything was intense, laid bare. A feeling of utter freedom. Limitless, unfiltered. Beauty, poverty, inequality. Obvious prostitution: all sexes, all ages.

Homosexuality lived in hiding. Very few Cambodians flaunted it in broad daylight. The general mindset was still steeped in traditional values, exerting tremendous social pressure as a result. The face shown to the world was a discreet gay scene made up of a few bars with moneyboys and ladyboys looking for foreign sugar daddies. Among the (s)expats, plenty of White Frenchmen. They maintained an ambiguous relationship with the locals, teetering between reverence and paternalism. Diasporic Cambodians now back in the homeland were but especially coveted. We were seen as representing the 'best of both worlds': an Asian phenotype and

Western culture. The myth of the banana—yellow on the outside, white on the inside—but not pejorative. Frenchmen in the gay microcosm pursued me with no subtlety whatsoever.

But I had eyes only for Khmers and was spoiled for choice. Gorgeous men on every street corner. Those bodies, that skin, those smiles! Was I myself succumbing to the eroticization of local boys? I couldn't deny that I felt certain fascination for them. But the (s)expats were already trying to teach me life lessons: *You can get your rocks off with Khmers, but if you're looking for something serious, forget it. Unless you want to keep shelling out. And even then, you won't have much to show for it, you'll have your fill and get bored.* They themselves complained that all Cambodians were only after their wallets and their dicks. They couldn't satisfy them all. I found their whingeing pathetic. Though their self-importance was nauseating, they were impossible to avoid. Phnom Penh was a village; everyone knew each other, ran into each other all the time. So I continued to see them socially, while setting a few rules for myself:

No sleeping with (s)expats

Exceptions: tourists and businessmen just passing through

Cambodians come first.

At the Blue Chilli Bar, one of Phnom Penh's oldest gay institutions, I was having a drink with a group of Frenchmen when I spotted an attractive Cambodian. We exchanged glances, smiles. We struck up a conversation. I learned that he was studying architecture. I found him interesting, charming. He excused himself for a moment. A Frenchman spoke up: *So you're talking with that whore? I banged him for twenty bucks! You've got good taste, he's a good lay.*

Later, I met a young Cambodian. He was working as an assistant for an NGO. We left for the southern province of Kep with a group of friends. We split all the costs—my obsession with equality again. While the others rented a villa, we stayed in a basic guesthouse, eating street food and rarely stepping out. He couldn't afford to do much more. We'd meet up with the Frenchmen and their Cambodian lovers at the rented villa. The Khmers played in the pool while the *barang*s[5] sipped their cocktails on deckchairs. I joined my lover, wrapped my arms around him; we lounged about, flirting and frolicking together in the pool. One of the Frenchmen commented: *What in the world are you doing with a Cambodian when you could have a Frenchman like me?*

C'mon, lucking into a Frenchman would be the Grail, right? Who cares if he doesn't look like much, if he spends his days plastered, ogling local ass and drooling, if he makes a living from shady deals and government handouts palmed on the sly, if he's more a wreck than a catch, if he washed up on these shores putatively to *aid development* when in reality he was a maladjusted misfit in France who hadn't found anywhere else to run aground? He'd still be better than any local—all Cambodians were good for was a cheap fuck. What you can't have, you must put down. *Slut. Whore. Bad in bed. Stuck up.* That's probably what they were saying behind my back.

My affair with the young Cambodian ended in stinging defeat after a few weeks. The gap between us—cultural and financial—proved too wide. All that stuff about equality was just hot air. An

---

5 In Khmer, a Frenchman, and thus, by extension, White.

imbalance of power persisted, and it wasn't a matter of colour. In such cases, social status won out over issues of race. I hated to admit it, but those vicious tongue waggers hadn't been entirely wrong. This time, at least. I was convinced I could find a happier ending with others. But the musical's run was drawing to a close.

I tried to stay in Cambodia, but my personal life was a rollercoaster. I was a nervous wreck, always on edge. Every time I'd begin to find my footing, all my landmarks would get blown to smithereens. Pay for sex—why not? See one boy, or several at a time—so what? I didn't burden myself with morality; any sense of framework or structure had gone out the window. It was time for me to make some hard decisions again. If I stayed here, I might hit rock bottom. But France? I didn't feel like going back. Banking? Out of the question. What if I had a go at an artistic career? Rediscovered the wonder of creative endeavour, the rush of being onstage? I had a little nest egg; I could hold out for a while. My financial-analysis professor had been right. Might as well put my ill-gotten gains to good use.

I flew to New York for a few months of intensive training in musical theatre, then landed a lead in a production in Los Angeles. The life of my dreams was still going strong. I'd gladly have stayed in the US to make it an American dream. But I felt that this was the right time to head back to France. No pressure, no obligation, no tail between my legs. I just wanted to pursue my apprenticeship, keep growing my artistic career. And what better place than Paris, 'the cultural capital of the world'?

9

Autumn 2009: the prodigal son returned. I pictured myself joining the big family of French cinema and live theatre. Bringing the house down in the nation's finest venues. Working with directors like Jacques Audiard, François Ozon, or even Abdellatif Kechiche. Winning an award—why not? I enrolled in acting classes at a performing arts centre on the outskirts of Paris. I needed to firm up my basics, acculturate myself to theatre, build a network. I figured: I can sing, I can dance, I can act, I speak lots of languages, and I've already played the lead in the US of A! As slam poet and lyricist Grand Corps Malade declaimed: *Obligé, ça peut chémar*! This was in the bag!

Plaine Saint-Denis studio, in the northern suburbs of Paris. The first audition I scored, for a presenter in a TV show: *Once more from the top, with an Asian accent*? Which one? *Whichever one you want, it doesn't matter*. Why does the presenter have an accent? *It's funny, we're just making fun. C'mon, time's a-wasting*! Go on. Again, *with more accent*! Reluctantly, I did as I was asked. I felt soiled, ridiculous. I was offered the role and told there'd be no pay. *It's a terrific opportunity, you'll be on TV and get some exposure*. No thanks, I'll pass.

Another audition, one for a musical after my voice demo had made it through pre-screening. In the hallway outside, I was the only non-White person. The casting director burst from the room and called my name. I rose and made my way towards him. When we were face to face, he looked me up and down and said, *Oh, right, OK.* I wilted on the spot. I knew right then and there it was pointless. Why bother even going in and warbling a tune? Still, I had to see things through, pro forma. Don't make a scene, don't discredit yourself.

Obviously, being an actor is being judged, scrutinized, criticized nonstop. Baring yourself, stripping down, putting your best foot forward, making yourself attractive. It takes a thick skin—armoured, even. But those looks, that disdain—I knew exactly what they meant: an Asian wouldn't cut it. It was the same look the bouncer at a gay club had given me before spitting out: *Not you.* I couldn't help but see similarities between my time on the gay scene and my experience as an actor.

In both cases, I came out of the gate raring and ready to conquer the world. Sure, I wasn't in the first blush of youth, I wasn't anyone's idea of a classical beauty, and at the tender age of thirty, I was already bald. But I figured I wasn't the ugliest either, nor the least talented, and that my particularities made me unique; I'd stand out from the crowd. My eyes full of stars, I was ready to meet all sorts of amazing people and have incredible experiences.

A profile on a dating site would catch my eye. I'd read the man's description of what he was looking for and think: *Hey, that's me!* I'd reach out: no answer. Or when an answer did come, it was always: *Sry, no Asians.* An ad on a casting site would catch my eye. I'd read the description of what they were after and think: *Hey, that's me!* I'd send in my headshot: no answer. Or when an answer did come, it was always: *Sry, no Asians.*

I couldn't believe it at first. *No, this just can't be! It's almost 2010, and this is still happening?!* I kept trying, just to convince myself I wasn't paranoid. And then it'd hit me, smack in the face: the whole *scene* didn't want me. Asians were neither sexy nor universal. Except maybe when it came to embodying a stereotype: in showbiz, they had to speak with accents and only play clichéd, ridiculous, or pathetic roles, lowly or unimportant. When it came to sex, they had to be passive, hairless, and submissive.

Anger always followed. I played the rebel, the bigmouth: I'd never talk with an accent! I'd never date someone with yellow fever! I'd never be a Gaysian slut (but just a slut? Sure, why not?)! I refused to conform to clichés. I wanted to be chosen for my personality, my talent—for *me*, goddammit!

Tired of storming off or being rejected, I made one concession, then two, then three. Out of convenience, practicality, laziness, weariness. *A man's gotta eat . . . Fine, but I was drunk . . . OK, fine, but he was sooo hot . . .* And later, I'd pray those compromising videos never turned up: shitty lay, shitty commercial. And if they did, well, I'd just have to own up to it.

Then I'd get a little schizophrenic: refusing to be picked for my background, I got myself an agent who specialized in 'Asian talent', while my profile on PlanetRomeo was literally: JneAsiat94 (YngAzn94: I could still get away with 'young' because you know what they say: Asians don't raisin; and 94 referred to the Val-de-Marne, the French department or quarter where I lived). I was way past being a contradiction.

Out of cynicism, resignation, or both, I indulged my depravity even further. For auditions and dating sites alike, I only searched for keywords now, exclusively picking ads and profiles containing the word *Asian*. There weren't many. Anything outside of that left me wary. Like that time when I was coming up from the subway and a good-looking young man stopped and smiled at me. I hurried off, panicked (*He couldn't have been smiling at me!*). Or that time when I was supposed to play a White woman's husband and wasn't convincing because I couldn't convince myself (*No one'll buy me in this role!*). I went so far as to develop paranoid tendencies and attribute my lack of success to my features. I didn't even try out any more if they weren't looking specifically for Asians. Waste of time. Waste of energy. In reality, I was doing their work for them and sabotaging myself, having come to believe I'd never be picked for anything else besides being Asian. And subtly, without my even noticing, the exception became the rule. That was all I did now. Being an Asian was my trademark and my stock-in-trade. I was disgusted with myself.

I tried my best to fit into the skin prescribed, until one day, a seam came loose. I pulled myself together, adjusted my goals. This time, I was more clear-sighted (or disillusioned, some might say, but drop it for now). Likely as not, I'd never get to go out with the kind of guy you see on magazine covers, no more than I'd ever get a close-up of my face on a movie poster. And I could live with that.

By saying no to being a clichéd bit part, I began to explore desires that were particular to me.

And it turned out pretty well. I wrote my first play. Not because I couldn't find the parts I deserved, as other actors who've gone into writing often claim. I'd had it up to here with the way Cambodians were portrayed, and I wanted to make my voice heard, to tell our story from the inside. I had so much to say. A Parisian theatre put on the show; I assembled a cast and improvised my way through directing them. I met more and more people who shared the same worldview, people I hit it off with as artists and human beings. I toured, acted, directed. I finally got contract status in the entertainment industry (state-certified in France) and could make a living from acting, unlike many others, some of whom had been in the business for longer. Opportunities came up, one gig followed another. It was what economists call a virtuous circle. As good gatekeepers, insiders wondered about my presence. But I was now used to being seen as an anomaly, and no longer wasted time explaining myself.

10

One way I made a living was doing drag queen numbers at the Tango, a Parisian nightclub whose owner was a friend. One night in the fall of 2010, he threw a dinner party. Among those invited was a mystery guest I hadn't been told about. I soon saw it was a trap. The mama-san, as he liked to call himself, liked to play matchmaker. I was enraged. Since when had I needed anyone to fix me up? To top it all off, the boy in question had just broken up with a Korean. He was into Asians. I snubbed him all night, being as obnoxious as I knew how. My first instinct was to reject him. According to my logic, if he'd already gone out with Asians—worse yet, if he'd *only ever* gone out with Asians—that meant he collected them, which made him a fetishist.

But then I wondered: why was that so bad? Could you judge, or even condemn someone on the basis of their past romances? In reality, was I the one doing the excluding, leaping to conclusions? Wasn't I myself guilty of internalized racism? After all, each one of his exes had a name, a personality, a story, and here I was, denying them any individuality, sweeping them all into categories I looked down on: Asian, sellout, potato queen. I also came to ask myself if those I deemed Asiaphiles didn't in fact have a sharper eye when it came to telling us apart, discerning our particularities, than those to whom we all looked alike. Wouldn't their gaze work like that of certain specially trained AI programs? There'd been an article in the Quebecois publication *CScience* on biases found in the mechanisms of facial recognition tools: 'The main facial recognition programs have a margin of error of less than 1% for White men vs. 35% for Black women.'[6]

Not because machines were establishing any racial hierarchies, or because White people were more readily identifiable and distinguishable, but because the human programmers were supplying far more data and photos of White men, which enabled the AI to differentiate them more effectively. This model of information assimilation resembles the one at work in our brains. The more data our brains sock away, the more nuances they can appreciate. In short, whether machine or human, we are taught how to see things and can get better at it. If all Asians look alike to you, maybe you haven't seen enough of them. And the reverse: if you pay more attention to a specific population, are you more able to recognize its specificities?

I myself had borne the cost of such confusion. At one conference I'd attended, several people came up to congratulate me for taking the floor the night before. The thing was, I hadn't been there the night before, and the man who had given a speech was fifty-something, tall, and olive-skinned, with glasses and a full head of hair. Naturally, my initial reaction was to be offended. How could

---

6 Caroline Lefer-Palos, 'L'IA est-elle raciste?' [Is AI racist?], *CSscience*, 13 July 2020: https://bit.ly/3JWdJEN.

they ever have mistaken us for each other? We had nothing in common! It was blindingly obvious! I should add that my congratulators were Black, from various Francophone African countries. But was it really racism? Or just bias from a lack of familiarity on their part?

The same thing goes for romantic liaisons. No one wants to be confused with someone else. We all want to feel unique. But if fetishists find *all* Asians intrinsically desirable, could it be that to a lover, *each one* is desirable for different reasons? The line between fetishism and preference is blurry and porous. To tell one person from another, you have to make an effort, not reject them all wholesale. And if you ask someone else to show discernment, you can't exempt yourself from doing the same.

Several months later, I ran into the man from the dinner party on a dating site. We began chatting. In the end, he wasn't such a bad sort. Quite the opposite. We made a date for a drink at the Duplex, a bar we both liked. There was a spark. He made me laugh. I found him endearing. I never got bored. He was quiet by nature, and his presence calmed me. We complemented each other. Little by little, I fell for his charms. We introduced each other to all of our respective friends, supported each other—he in my artistic career, I in his attempts to found a company. We wound up moving in together. Meanwhile, I'd made progress and settled into my relationship with Cambodia. The country was now an integral part of my life and identity. I could deal with being loved for that side of me *too*.

Having both been defectors in our personal journeys, we saw eye to eye. But not on everything. When the issue of race found its way into our personal and social interactions, things got muddy. Because he couldn't see it, hadn't experienced the same things. When I'd get stopped in airports, my papers checked, my luggage rifled through—which never happened to him—he'd chalk it up to chance, *random* inspections. When we were on vacation and I'd constantly get snubbed, he'd either deny it (*It's all in your head!*), or else minimize it (*Calm down. Why can't you just let it go?*), which only exasperated me more. Enjoying the privilege of ignorance, he lived in a state of denial.

On a three-week trip to Sri Lanka, I grew tired of explaining myself and said only this: *Watch closely.* We moved around the island from one town to another every few days. Getting out of the car, at hotels, in restaurants, at tourist sites, it was the same scene over and over—there was no shortage of examples. At dinner, when the waiter would pull out his chair and hold out the menu (while ignoring me, naturally), I'd see his face suddenly change: *Again? I can't believe this!* In his eyes, I saw anger, incomprehension, the loss of innocence. I just hoped he wouldn't make a scene; it would've been more embarrassing than anything else. I didn't need a saviour. He couldn't pretend not to notice any more—that was already something.

Such actions do not necessarily denote overt racism. Unpleasant as they are, they could merely reflect patterns and habits. In the case of Sri Lanka, international tourists are still mostly White. East and Southeast Asians are few and far between. Surely there's some automatic association: the White man has the money, makes the decisions, speaks English. As for the *other* one, well, we're not too sure who he is and how to deal with him, so let's just ignore him.

And yet the entire time we travelled together, no matter where we went, we were never subjected to homophobia. Two grown men sharing a room left little doubt as to our sexual identity. As a gay couple, we used to feel more at ease and safer in hotels billed as *gay friendly*; otherwise we would be forced to be more discreet. But now, no matter where we go, the staff of any establishment wouldn't raise an eyebrow despite what they might personally think of us. If heteros and homos can enjoy the same treatment today, then maybe it can be that way for Whites and non-Whites someday too. It will require educating people about faces, depictions, representations. I'm talking about the hospitality industry here, the service sector, but such education will have to spread to all social and institutional spheres.

When I'm faced with a genuinely hostile, even aggressive attitude, I never hesitate to point it out, complain to management, or leave a murderous review online. My partner used to try and temper such behaviour out of embarrassment. After that trip, he stood by my side in silent support. Over time, I pretended to be less annoyed. It wasn't my job to educate everyone I met. We learned to defuse situations before they became disagreeable, even laugh at them. We couldn't allow them to poison our relationship.

That relationship lasted for five years of ups and downs. Then, more downs than ups, with more and more fights. One night, we had to face facts: we weren't happy any more. Better to break it off.

We spent the rest of the night reminiscing fondly about our time together. At dawn, I packed my things.

The breakup coincided with my decision to put an end to my artistic activities. A few months earlier, I'd wrapped up a show that had been the culmination of over a year's work, one that I'd adapted for the stage, directed, starred and produced. Even though on the verge of exhaustion, I went on with rehearsals for a role in the musical *The King and I*. Despite an acerbic op-ed I'd penned on Lambert Wilson landing the role of the King of Siam, as soon as a spot opened up in the cast, I rushed to fill it. We put on eight shows a week. I felt like a machine. Here I was, in an opulent big-budget production at the lavish Théâtre du Châtelet, and I took no joy from it whatsoever.

Once the run had wrapped, I started down a slippery slope. I scoured the ads looking for gigs, obsessed solely with renewing my contract-worker status. The offerings seemed less and less interesting, increasingly commercial. My heart was no longer in it. Worn out by my previous project, I didn't have the strength to start a new one. Above all, I didn't feel like forcing myself to stage a show or write another play. I didn't want to end up like those people who didn't know when to quit and just kept going, into bitterness and artistic impoverishment, convinced it was all they knew how to do. If I had nothing left to say, I would rather be silent and make my exit. My decision met with disbelief from all parts: *You're making a living in a field where tons of other people are struggling to scrape by! You found your passion! You're one of the few Asians representing us out there!*

I've always been surprised by the expectations projected on me. As an artist, I had a particular responsibility when it came to the Asian community at large, especially since I'd made a public stand more than once against anti-Asian discrimination. Some saw me as a defender of the cause and wanted me to respond to every occasion. But no matter what I did, it was either too much or not enough. On one hand, whenever I didn't speak up, it was held against me: *We missed you during the Kev Adams controversy!*[7] On the other, when I did express myself on social issues, that was held against me as well: *Your path as an artist has taken a political turn.* To a certain extent, I understand how the lack of public figures of Asian descent can give rise to all sorts of expectations. You hang onto whoever might be a spokesperson. But that was a role I refused to play and gladly ceded to others.

And thus, once again, I wiped the slate clean, ready to plug a few quarters in the machine and try my luck, starting over from scratch.

Reset.

Play.

---

7 *Le Parisien*, 'Sketch sur les "Chinois": accusé de racisme, Gad Elmaleh s'explique' [Accused of racism in his sketch about 'Chinese' people, comedian Gad Elmaleh offers an explanation], *Le Parisien*, 24 April 2018: https://bit.ly/3DthVIN.

III

1

In November 2015, France was stunned by the bloody terrorist attacks all over Paris. I was alone in my studio in Arcueil during these traumatic events. No partner, no projects, no prospects. My contract-worker status in the entertainment industry was coming to an end, and I was about to go on welfare. Total fail. To top it all off, I was back on the meat market. It was now the age of apps, and Grindr reigned supreme. But the scene was still the same pitiful, depressing mess. Worse, even, for the bell had tolled: I was about to turn thirty-five, the expiration date for a gay man. Past that milestone, you were officially old. I used to be able to pass vaguely for a *young Asian*, at least. Now I was an *old Asian*, good for nothing but the scrap heap. Even rice queens gave me the cold shoulder.

PrEP[1] had just hit the scene, and riding bareback was becoming popular. The idea sickened and repelled me. My generation had come of age fearing AIDS and thinking of condoms as a must. I'd always managed to require them of myself and of others; the thought of doing without them never crossed my mind. Until one day when, carried away on a wave of excitement, I had a moment of weakness. The guy said he was *clean* and came on pretty hard. I

---

1 Pre-Exposure Prophylaxis is an antiretroviral treatment that reduces one's chances of getting HIV from sex or injection drug use.

gave in. As soon as it was over, I was overcome by panic. How could I take the word of someone I'd just met an hour ago? If he was doing this with me, that meant he'd done it with others. He could've been HIV-positive and just didn't know it himself. Worse yet, he could've been a *gift giver*, one of those infected people who go around deliberately spreading disease! The risks were real. I thought about going to the ER. In the end, I did nothing. Simply spent twelve weeks worrying myself sick before I could take a screening. The results were negative. Relieved, I vowed never to let such a thing happen again. But a few weeks later, it did.

Was I flirting with death, or had I found a way to feel alive? Surely there was something exciting about this transgression. Still, my game of Russian roulette had me reeling with anxiety. I couldn't take it any more. But instead of getting a hold of myself, I started PrEP.

I became a fan of unprotected sex. Every three months, at a follow-up visit, I'd be diagnosed with new STIs. Infection, treatment, infection, treatment . . . I kept piling on ever shadier and shittier sexual encounters. One morning, I woke up to find my face swollen, my eyes bloodshot, my tongue on fire, and my limbs throbbing. Every last part of my body was in pain. Upon leaving the house, I collapsed in the middle of the street. Despite endless exams, the doctors came up with nothing. I wasn't sick or suffering from medicinal side effects. It was all psychosomatic. My inner wounds were getting infected. Suddenly, the wounds I thought had healed over for good were opening up once more. How could I keep mutilating myself like this?

2

Little by little, I emerged from the hole I'd crawled into. As idleness hadn't suited me, I devoted my meagre energies to resuming my professional activities. My new direction was training and teaching. I scraped by between contract gigs and unemployment, loneliness and hook-ups. But I put an end to PrEP and risky sex. I had to heed the signals my body was sending me, for fear of my life. The desire for travel overtook me again. I fixated on Taiwan, a country I'd loved so much after visiting with friends from there. Scraping together my last few francs, I decided to go study Mandarin in Taipei in the summer of 2016.

Taipei wasn't especially pretty as cities go. Dense, vertical, concrete all over. But once past first impressions, I found it had a peculiar charm, an atmosphere I'd never come across anywhere else. This was due in large part to the people. There was a social intelligence, a striking civility, especially compared with the every-man-for-himself jungle of Paris, where you had to fight tooth and nail for every square inch of personal space, and your fellow human beings were seen as invaders. Paris made me aggressive. I was constantly on my toes. And just when I least expected it, the racist insults, the ridicule, the petty queries, the dark looks would come my way.

I knew better, but I'd still be caught off guard. A rent-a-cop at the entrance to the college where I was teaching: *Ni hao!* A woman in the metro: *Go back home, you dirty slope!* A dinner with friends: *No, I meant 'Laos-y', not 'lousy'!*

In Taiwan, this burden was lightened. No one gave me a second glance. In Singapore and Phnom Penh, I was singled out, if only for how I dressed or carried myself, my way of moving. In Taipei, no one could tell I wasn't local until I opened my mouth. I who'd always liked standing out from the crowd now sampled the luxury of invisibility. It was so relaxing! I could finally be done with all that *race* business. Taiwan as a nation didn't seem obsessed by the issue, and when it came up in conversation, the Taiwanese were satisfied with any answer I gave, instead of poking and prodding at it (*Oh, really? Well, I would've thought that . . .*). As part of the majority, I represented the universal standard. Paradoxically, among the masses, all our distinctive features re-emerged: you could be an individual and seen as such by one and all. These few months did me a world of good. I had a torrid affair with a seductive Sino-Malaysian journalist and began to believe that meaningful relationships were still possible.

During my time in Taiwan, something happened in France that would prove a tipping point for society. In August 2016, Zhang Chaolin, a Chinese tailor of modest income, sustained fatal injuries during a violent mugging in the middle of the street in the northern Paris suburb of Aubervilliers. Nor was this the first such incident to make France's many Asian communities feel unsafe. Criminals regularly target Asians, seeing them as walking moneybags, encouraged by the myth of the rich Chinese man who goes out for a stroll with a wad of cash and won't lift a finger to defend himself. Among certain gangs, *bagging a Chinaman* even amounts to a rite of passage.[2] Others want to prove their strength by attacking a so-called black belt. In reality, victims of such aggressions are most often women, the elderly, or those who look harmless, like Zhang Chaolin, who at forty-nine was young for a grandfather. His death, on top of the consternation and despair of Asians in France, lack of action on the government's part, and silence in the media, led to protests of over 10,000 strong, for the most part Asian—a first for a population reputedly so quiet and unassuming.

This was also the start of public allegations of anti-Asian racism. Previously, this had not been discussed much, and many persisted in denying its existence. Cries of anger and exasperation rang out every which way. Accusations of violence and discrimination surfaced in every area from the professional to the artistic, personal safety to interpersonal relations. We wanted to be acknowledged like any other citizen, or simply as human beings. We'd had enough of being seen as emotionless machines, robots whose sole function was labour. We understood that being deemed well-integrated immigrants offered no protection whatsoever. That in fact by viewing us in this way, the French were being not only reductive but blowing smoke, and the wind could change at any

---

2 Denis Courtine et Fanny Delporte, 'Vitry: Les agressions contre les Asiatiques se multiplient à nouveau' [Anti-Asian aggression on the rise again in Vitry], *Le Parisien*, 16 May 2019: https://bit.ly/46LA9Cp.

moment—we could go from being a model minority to a problematic one. The Covid-19 pandemic that led to a flare-up in violence against anyone perceived as Asian in certain Western countries such as France, the US, and Canada was a painful wake-up call. In the collective imagination, all Asians were Chinese, and stigmatized as a result.

In the wake of this movement of affirmation and assertion, another struggle was mounted: to expose clichés about Asians of all sexes. That was what blogger Grace Ly undertook to do with her web series *Ça reste entre nous* [Just between us]. The first episode, shot in early 2017, interrogated the image of the Asian woman[3] by giving voice to four French women of Chinese, South Korean, Cambodian, and Laotian descent. Despite the term *Asian*, this was mostly about East and Southeast Asia, and excluded the rest of the continent, as is often the case when in France. The women tackled profound topics in an easygoing way: identity, biculturalism, mixed-race relationships, and discrimination.

The second episode concerned the image of the Asian man[4] and was much the same. Three guests discussed masculinity, love lives, dating, and representation. I'd known Grace Ly for a few years, and we'd planned for me to be a part of this episode. I'd liked the pilot and was into the idea of making an appearance. But a few days before filming was to begin, I took a powder. I would've

---

3 Ca Reste Entre Nous Officiel, 'L'image de la femme asiatique', *YouTube*, 20 February 2017: https://youtu.be/TSmiEcyWW8c.

4 Ca Reste Entre Nous Officiel, 'L'image de l'homme asiatique', *YouTube*, 18 September 2017: https://youtu.be/RoIGo3XMmeo.

had to talk about my specific life experiences as a gay man. While I didn't hide it, I took care not to mention my homosexuality openly. Moreover, I never understood why high-profile figures systematically had their homosexuality specified with such labels as *gay* singer, *gay* journalist, *gay* parliamentarian—was all that really necessary? For me, it was an invasion of the private sphere. That was, at least, the reason I gave for turning down the invitation to appear. In truth, I was paralysed by my old nemeses: fear and shame. What if a family member happened upon the broadcast? What if it hurt my career? What if it made me a target for homophobic attacks?

A few months later, the 'Yellow Is Beautiful'[5] campaign was launched across social networks, its aim to *reveal the beauty of Asian men*. Once again, it was just about East Asia—that's what *yellow* referred to. As the word was often pejorative in French, here they sought to flip the stigma with a pale imitation of the 'Black is Beautiful' movement. The AJ+ network from Al Jazeera made a short video report[6] that featured a portrait session followed by an interview with the photographer and some of the participants. The initiative had taken shape in response to rejections some of these men had experienced from women. The intention was to set things straight by showing that *Asian men can be handsome and virile*.

Under the pretext of diversifying beauty, the men selected matched up perfectly with a stereotypical, testosterone-swollen

---

5 'Yellow Is Beautiful', *Facebook*, 21 July 2017: https://bit.ly/3DaQDXl.

6 AJ+ français, 'L'art contre les clichés anti-Asiatiques' [Art against anti-Asian clichés], *Facebook*, 21 September 2019: https://bit.ly/46MK7U2.

representation of masculinity. Splashed across the page were muscles taut and bulging, abs sculpted and oiled, torsos tattooed, and, in some cases, hairy. At the end of the day, clichés were embodied rather than deconstructed. The benchmark was still outdated Western norms; we just wanted to show we could also be part of the club.

For the very concept of manliness is a hoax. It claims to establish what a man is, a *real* man—that is, an alpha male, a dominator, not a sissy, a conqueror, not a pansy. All it really does is impose harmful, oppressive standards on those concerned who, in the grip of a virile delirium, constantly try to outdo themselves. At the other end of the spectrum is the cliché of the sensitive, tender, attentive Asian man. He has become the incarnation of *soft* masculinity, his reputation restored. But not in everyone's eyes. He is only prized by ladies who fantasize about sweet, gentle men.

For many of us raised in France, the hit our pride took from this putative lack of manliness was long taken in stride. We seek to soothe our maimed egos by any means we can. When it comes to being attractive, we have two choices: jock or twink, pumping iron or plucking our eyebrows. If that's your thing, go for it! But make no mistake: we don't need to submit our masculinity or features to others for their approval. We don't need to go begging them for validation or legitimacy. Beauty is found everywhere, in all of us. It's up to us to bring it to light. Through our own eyes, on our own terms.

3

Back in France in the autumn of 2016, I noticed a change: anti-Asian discrimination was finally attracting some notice. Even *Têtu*, the leading gay magazine, was getting into it, running the story 'Do gays have a problem with fat peoples?'[7] with the following intro: ' "No femmes, no fats, no Asians!" is all over our dating apps. Where does this aversion towards minorities in the gay community come from?'

I wasn't a regular reader, but as far I knew, this was the first time that periodical had tackled head-on the rejection Asians faced in the gay scene. It was a mini-revolution, and I had high hopes. At last, the scope and origins of this phenomenon would be revealed. But only one paragraph in the article raised the issue of Asians: 'Being fat is seen as being both weak and feminine. Hence the double-barreled "No fats / No femmes" and even "No Asians", for Asians often have a different cultural construct of manliness.'

While linking fatness and femininity left me dubious, I found the explanation about Asians frankly distressing. We were being

---

7 Jérémy Patinier, 'Enquête: les gays ont-ils un problème avec les gros?' [Study: Do gays have a problem with fat people?], *Têtu*, 18 October 2016: https://bit.ly/3PSjZ48.

rejected due to a 'different cultural construct of manliness'? What was the author talking about? As he hadn't bothered to further develop his point, what he might have meant was left to my imagination.

One might indeed observe what seem like inarguable differences between East and West when it comes to expressing virility. For example, in Korean and Japanese dramas, men are often of sensitive and delicate character. In South Korean K-Pop, the ideal of male beauty is a young man in an eye-popping getup with an over-the-top hairdo. The frequent use of make-up reinforces this closeness to femininity. It is thus common to imagine Asian men as affected and androgynous, as such images are abundantly disseminated by East Asian pop culture, with its 'global' reach. In South and Southeast Asian countries, men are much more touchy-feely. One might also point to the Indian *hijra* or *kinnar* (intersex, eunuchs, or transgender) and the Thai *kathoey* or *phuying*, which pose more ambiguous and complex representations of gender and are sometimes perceived as a *third sex*, though nonbinary conceptions of gender can be found in other cultures and peoples throughout the world.

This handful of examples show that cultural specificities do indeed exist, but are they representative of Asia as a whole? Do we imagine that music videos and TV series reflect reality? That certain marginal and often marginalized gender categories are the norm? At any rate, the issue cannot be a 'different cultural construct of manliness', as the article suggests. Deploying this argument

to explain anti-Asian discrimination merely intensifies the stigma-
tization. It places responsibility for rejection squarely upon us, the
victims. It confirms the authors in their beliefs, for it implies that
we are indeed less virile, not because of our nature—that is, the
physical characteristics we supposedly share—but because of our
culture: so which one is it? Who knows? It presumes that people
who look Asian on apps are culturally Asian and not European. In
so doing, it blithely annihilates the experience of French people of
Asian descent, the first to bear the consequences of such sexual
racism. Will someone please tell me how my own cultural construct
of manliness is so different from that subscribed to by everyone
else in France?

But don't go telling me that in Asian countries (which are
many and very different each from the next) androgyny is common,
men wear make-up, cross-dress, or live out trans lives in a very natural, fluid fashion, accepted by the whole of society. Don't go telling
me that men there, especially homosexuals, shape their personality
according to standards so very different from those found in the
West. *Au contraire*, I'll reply: in many a gay Asian scene, the cult of
the toned body and normative pressure are *exactly* the same as they
are in the West.

Don't believe me? All you have to do is pop over for a visit,
travel the various countries on the continent, stroll through the
cities and villages. See for yourself if the image of the 'Asian man'
exists. You'll note that manliness is expressed in more or less the
same way, even its most harmful and toxic aspects. Our ethnocentric

gaze is responsible for this projection of otherness, which ends up being all we can see. Either a fantasized ideal: *Asia is so much more progressive on these issues*! Or open contempt: *Asia—what a cream-puff factory*! Instead of looking for difference at any cost, we would do better to interrogate our own representations. And if the standards of masculinity are starting to be called into question, this is more of a generational phenomenon, worldwide rather than confined to a specific geographical area.

A few weeks later, I read an article on Slate.fr titled 'I believed the gay scene would be spared from racism. I was soon disillusioned.'[8] It provided a more detailed and pertinent overview of the issue (*Têtu* would soon rush to catch up with other pieces on the same theme):

> There's no shortage of such stories, especially when 'No Blacks, no Asians' floods the statuses of many dating apps and site users. 'Dating and sex are some of the last parts of life where people just won't own up to discrimination,' laments David, a twenty-seven-year-old man originally from Toulouse.

David's experience leads the reporter to muse:

> How to explain the grip racism has on the homosexual community? Beyond systemic racism, perhaps a postcolonial sexual and erotic imagination is still busy influencing us.

---

8 Florian Bardou, 'Je pensais que le milieu gay serait épargné par le racisme. J'ai vite déchanté', *Slate*, 18 November: https://bit.ly/44Dmrjg.

A study performed in 2009 and again in 2014 by the American dating site OkCupid prompted reflection on racial discrimination in the romantic sphere.[9] Their statistics revealed the least sought-out categories to be Asian men and Black women, while the most desirable were White men and Asian women.

Another study conducted in the United Kingdom in 2015 by *FS Magazine*, the gay and bisexual men's health periodical from The Fact Site, focused on discrimination against ethnic minorities among gays:[10]

In the FS 'Racism on the scene survey':

80% of Black guys,

79% of Asian guys,

75% of South Asian guys,

64% of mixed-race guys

and most of the Arab guys who responded said they've personally experienced racism on Britain's gay scene.

Some of the stories were common: many recalled being ignored on the scene or being blocked or called racist names on apps. For some the racial abuse went much deeper.

---

9 Sofi Papamarko, 'Why Black Women and Asian Men Are at a Disadvantage When It Comes to Online Dating', *Toronto Star*, 21 March 2017: https://bit.ly/3pJJXfK.

10 Stuart Haggas, 'Racism and the Gay Scene', *LGBT Hero*, n.d.: https://bit.ly-/44B286F.

While these studies definitely got things moving, they still remained American and British conversations. Then they hit France, affecting hetero- and homo-spheres. It became increasingly difficult to claim you didn't see colour. It was time to admit that race as a factor played a genuine role in our choice of romantic and sexual partners.

Until that moment, all this had merely been anecdotal for me, personal experience; now, such observations and intuitions were statistical fact, documented and plainly stated. I, too, began talking to friends of Asian descent and realized that *everyone* had faced the same kind of discrimination in their romantic lives. Each of us, alone in our corners, had endured such unpleasantness yet never opened up about it. As if none of it were serious. We all just made do. Or didn't. Suddenly, I realized something: we weren't so much a community bound by ethnicity as a community bound by experience based on the way that ethnicity had been perceived. In a way, we could indeed claim brotherhood. Brotherhood of hardship.

4

The early autumn of 2016 was going well. I'd picked up a number of teaching gigs at universities, companies, and organizations, and was making a decent living. I'd gotten into badminton, made new friends, and was continuing to work on my Mandarin. Life had resumed its course.

The holidays were fast approaching. An artist of Chinese-Cambodian descent I knew well invited me and a few other close friends over for cocktails and dinner. I was introduced to his former art-school prof and her partner, a White couple in their sixties. There was also another couple, in their thirties, a French-Cambodian woman and her husband, also White. If I've stipulated their race—social, not biological—it's because this element is far from inconsequential to what follows. Wine, cheese, cured meats: everything was going well. We talked merrily about this and that. Until Asia entered the conversation.

The professor told us about her trip to South Korea as part of a cultural exchange programme. She described a backward, patriarchal society where women were oppressed, horrified yet marvelling as she conjured up a scene she had witnessed. Right in the middle of the street, a woman was being beaten by a man identified as her husband until another teacher in the group, a *tall Swedish man*, intervened and shook up the *little Korean*. She went on, recalling a point on which her female Asian exchange students in France had all unanimously agreed: never would they date an Asian man. In fact, Asian men didn't want free, independent women. So the students tried to set themselves all up with native Frenchmen. The professor spoke of her female students with fervour, endorsing their work of *deconstruction*.

I ventured a joke: clearly, Asian men had nothing going for them. Not only were they neither manly nor attractive, but also old hat and sexist to boot! The joke fell flat. Stony faces stared back at me. I whetted my rebuttals and flung out a few: was violence towards women unique to Asian societies? In France, a woman died from domestic abuse every three days. How was dating a Frenchman any protection against violence or a warranty of better treatment? Did all Asian men behave the same way, share the same mindset? Wasn't asserting as much giving into essentialism, the very opposite of deconstructionism? Did the same apply to men of Asian descent born in France and raised in French—tar 'em all with the same brush and feather 'em too, while you're at it? The French-Cambodian woman joined the fray, adding: *It's not the same. Things are worse in Asia. Statistics on domestic violence in Papua New Guinea prove it.*

The debate raged on, but no one was really listening to each other any more. Facts no longer mattered. We were each representing our own group. Women vs Men. As women, they alone could pronounce on this subject. Anything I said lacked all legitimacy. I should shut up, unless I was agreeing with them. Offer condemnation. Even of myself. I felt like the defendant in court called to answer for the patriarchy whose avatar I had suddenly become. Instead, I was acting like the defender of the besmirched reputation of Asian men.

We monopolized the conversation, tearing into each other between bites of charcuterie. None of the other men spoke a word. They'd figured out their two cents weren't welcome. I wondered how my friend of Chinese-Cambodian descent felt about all this. What did the words *never with an Asian man* mean to him? Did he feel concerned, affected, targeted, wounded when they came not from strangers or anonymous commenters hiding behind a screen name, but instead blithely, from close friends? In me, they struck a nerve. But maybe I was too sensitive about such things?

I didn't know what to do any more, shut up or open up, watch my words or stick my foot in my mouth, de-escalate or threaten to ruin the evening. I'd expressed my disagreement at that infamous dinner, but by the end of the night, I felt guilty for making the atmosphere uncomfortable, so I excused myself and left. Which only exacerbated my frustration. Not only had I been upset by racist remarks, but I'd done my utmost not to embarrass everyone else.

Was the solution to a more peaceful, manageable social life only seeing people who shared my own experiences and ideas? The older I got, the more tempting that seemed. But instead of walling myself off, I thought I would seek an environment better suited to me, even if that meant yet another change of scene. What I did could be called running away, but I prefer to call it self-preservation. And unlike the Pet Shop Boys, who sang the praises of going west, for me, the exhortation was rather: Go East!

5

A news item on social media electrified me: a cultural NGO based in Cambodia that I'd worked with before was about to set up shop in Taipei, the city of my dreams. I got back in touch with the directors. With any luck, they'd be looking for someone to run the new branch. They informed me that a managerial position was indeed open, but . . . in Phnom Penh. I had a deep love for the Cambodian capital, but I'd never pictured myself going back to live there; a bitter taste lingered in my mouth from my previous abortive expatriation. The thought of being an employee again gave me anxiety. After tasting the freedoms of freelancing for over a decade, could I stand having a boss, co-workers, the workaday schedule again? My stomach was tied up in knots just thinking about sitting down to work every day at the same desk, seeing the same faces . . . But the NGO's mission seemed inspiring: developing the local artistic scene. It was an exciting professional challenge that would enable me to learn new skills. I applied for the job and, after a series of tests and interviews, it was offered to me. I cleared my calendar, ready to take off once more. Cambodia, here I come again!

What I discovered was a brand-new land, not even vaguely resembling the one I'd first encountered a dozen years earlier.

Highrises had shot up everywhere. Some neighbourhoods had coffee shops on every corner. The potholed streets swarmed with auto-rickshaws reservable by smartphone. Phnom Penh had climbed aboard the bandwagon of modernity and globalization, which wasn't at all to the taste of those nostalgic for a timeless Cambodia. The energy was palpable, a frenzy that surged through an exuberant younger generation, a new population of expats both Western and Asian, and many Cambodians from the diaspora who'd chosen to come back. (S)expats and other 'filth' no longer held centre stage. They'd retreated to a few streets and bars I no longer patronized.

Relationships between boys had changed radically. More and more Cambodians were proclaiming their pride in themselves and their attraction for their fellow men, flaunting their muscles on social media and living their best lives in broad daylight. The centre of gravity had shifted: no need for affirmation from an outside gaze now. Cambodians stood on their own two feet. Unless all this just meant they'd simply imported Western values and applied them to themselves? Was the only path to legitimacy, a sense of self-worth, through the cult of the body, activism, and Western-style affirmation?

Things were different for me in the country as well. The question of race stopped interfering in my private life. I didn't have to play the Asian any more, conform to expectations brought on by such fantasies. I could be anything, everything, and did not hesitate to explore new possibilities. I no longer experienced the act of sex as a battle to be won. It was a simple, natural pleasure. The way Cambodians looked at me gave me back my individuality.

I could dwell in my own body as I saw fit. Even the experience of sensuality was different. There was something more intimate, more familiar about sex. Something unique about the way of smelling (in Khmer, the word for 'kiss' is the word for 'sniff' or 'inhale'), touching, devouring each other. Obviously, this didn't apply to everyone. It was first and foremost about a connection between individuals. Chemistry and alchemy.

Up till then, I'd been used to comparisons, classifications, winners, always drawing subdivisions within each category: Whites vs Blacks, Africans vs Caribbeans, Martinicans vs Guadeloupeans, mixed-race vs *chabins*[11] . . . Or even Latinos vs Asians, East Asians vs South Asians, Vietnamese vs Cambodians, urban Chinese-Cambodians vs rural Khmers . . .

All that got smashed to pieces. After examining the issue from every angle, I came to this flippant conclusion: race does not a lover make. Moreover, my many hook-ups helped me demystify sex. Pleasure could be taken and given in many ways, and wasn't a matter of diameter. A cock did not a lover make, any more than race.

I learned as well that it was better to avoid mentioning, much less flaunting, your exes. Few could keep from comparing themselves. It was titillating to their ego, but rarely in a good way. It gave rise to repulsion, fantasies, complexes, especially when it came to Black men: *Doesn't their smell make you want to throw up? So is it true what they say about them? Sigh . . . you're going to find me disappointing. Once you go Black . . .* You had to handle these men with

---

11 In the French Antilles, a person with a very light complexion whose phenotypic features are reminiscent of a person of African descent.

kid gloves, constantly reassure them, spare their vulnerable virility. A man is a fragile thing.

To my great surprise, I bedded boys each more stunning than the last. Since most of my Cambodian encounters took place with a minimum of conversation, if any at all, I was within reason to doubt this was due to some prestige of my nationality or profession. My partners never asked me for anything in return. This happened often enough to convince me it wasn't random, or mere luck. Had I suddenly become more attractive in Cambodia?

My age might have had something to do with it. I was pushing forty and had never felt so good in my own skin before. Forty is the new twenty! Some found me virile, while others said they saw me as a *daddy*, both of which seemed like compliments. Moreover, my pale complexion, which I'd never liked, was a plus here. In Cambodia, light skin is considered beautiful, a mark of higher social status, while darker skin is disparaged. How often had I heard boys curse their olive skin, calling it *khmao*, or 'black' in Khmer? Interestingly enough, on Grindr, some of them selected *Black*, not *Asian*, as their ethnicity. In France, I thought of very good-looking men as out of my league and never even tried to approach them. I believe I was just being realistic and have no regrets. Still, I can't help but wonder what would've happened had I been bolder. Could what was happening to me in Cambodia be chalked up to less inhibition and regaining confidence in myself?

While I'd never been so sexually fulfilled before, romantically things were less gratifying. A doubt gnawed at me. What if I'd already found love once and let it slip away?

6

Two and a half years had passed since I'd moved to Cambodia and taken up a position at the cultural NGO. I'd never thought it would last this long. What seemed like a dream job had soon turned into a hellish cycle. My job was more about bureaucracy than artistic creation. I spent the better part of my days in meetings, answering emails, writing up reports. There were a thousand problems I had to tend to, a thousand fires to put out, always trying to do more with less. And yet I derived a certain satisfaction from it. I felt like I'd done my part, made my contribution. My efforts had been rewarded: I'd been promoted to associate director and would be transferred to Taipei before the summer. At last—Taiwan! There were a few months of transition left for training my successor, a young Cambodian woman who'd worked under me and was now rising through the ranks. What joy I felt, what pride! I left with peace in my heart.

In early 2020, a worrisome virus reared its head in Wuhan, China and swiftly spread. I was passing through France to turn in the keys for my studio in Arcueil. My first apartment. Where I'd sown my wild oats. It was time to part with it, say so long and thanks. But this wasn't about cutting ties with my motherland. Not completely, at least, since I'd come to celebrate my civil union. With the man who'd never left my thoughts. The whole time we'd been apart, I'd longed to have him back at my side.

At our reunion, he confessed he'd felt the same. We decided to give each other a second chance. And to keep from doing things halfway, we went directly from being exes to being civil partners. We were convinced we could make each other happy this time, and agreed to put in the work to make that happen. Despite all those who say getting back with a former lover is doomed to failure. Who say long-distance relationships never work out. Let them say what they want. We're not here to make liars of them, just to live our own lives. My partner, who had also fallen in love with Taiwan, planned on joining me there, at least for part of the year. For now, we were busy negotiating France and Cambodia, meeting up whenever our schedules allowed. Everything was falling into place. The picture was complete at last. I was entering a new stage in my life with utter serenity.

While in Paris, I went to the town hall of the fourth arrondissement for a panel about Asian LGBTQIA representation.[12] I had a special interest in what the panellists had to say: five young persons of Southeast Asian descent, all in their twenties—men, women, and trans. They spoke of the lack of role models for gays, lesbians, and trans people of Asian descent, of how this weighed on their mental and physical health and what repercussions it had, of their ties with

---

12 La Semaine LGBT Chinoise à Paris, 'Les personnes asiatiques LGBTQIA: quelles représentations?' [Asian LGBTQIA people: What representations?], *Facebook*, 28 January 2020: https://bit.ly/44F7r4j

their countries of origin. They spoke with such power and maturity, such bite.

I had a burning question that I finally got to ask at the end. I brought up the constant rejection I faced when I entered the gay scene in the '90s. Were they going through the same thing twenty years later? If so, what were they doing about it? They all had the same answer: the same intolerance, the same racism was still deeply embedded in the queer community. Their solution was to hang out only with non-Whites or members of their own ethnic group, to avoid the risk of being objectified or fetishized.

I was exasperated. Nothing had changed in two decades. But as I listened to them, I realized that this wasn't entirely true. I'd noticed changes. The young generation had conceptual weapons I hadn't had at my disposal, could put precise words to the mechanisms they were trying to dismantle. They could speak now of *safe spaces, intersectionality, decolonization, non-mixity, cisnormativity*. I do not deny that things must be correctly named, that the work of deconstruction includes deconstructing language. But I confess that I can't quite manage it. I find all these new concepts unwieldy, get lost in what is and isn't appropriate to say. As for inclusive writing—I don't really get how to deploy it, much less how to pronounce it.

Debates about race have gone public. Society is more receptive to them. Many voices are denouncing blatant racism on the gay scene and beyond. Grindr finally did away with ethnicity filters (even if, in the grand scheme of things, it didn't really change much about discriminatory practices). In my day, I was off alone in my corner struggling with all these matters for lack of a space in which to tackle them. I made do with slipping through the interstices. Today, *we don't agonize, we organize*, to paraphrase activist Florynce 'Flo' Kennedy's famous saying. Admittedly still from the fringes of society, but in a structured, deliberate way that we own up to. We're no longer apologizing, no longer trying to please. We've seceded from the patriarchy and White supremacy. I am struck by how radical the younger generation is, before remembering that I myself wasn't far from their stances. Though I understand the necessity of self-preservation, I still end up wondering how far back we should retreat. Aren't the circles we take refuge in ultimately a prison of our own choosing?

There are others who will no longer put up with life on the fringe. They want their slice of the pie—the best slice, even. They're not objecting to what's on menu, just to the fact of not having been invited to the table. Some retire from the game, others hope to win the match. Rarer still are those who try to change the rules. To them, the entire system must be reconceived from top to bottom. They put their heads together to question everything, in every sphere, every area. What was acceptable yesterday no longer is today. Previously unheard voices rise up in accusation and outrage, making demands, until every faction lets loose as virulently as possible. As far as I'm concerned, I'd rather not join in the cacophony. I'll lead a quiet life, away from the tumult. Maintain my precarious balance. Live in my own skin. That's a lot already.

Towards the end of my time in Paris, I had a drink with a friend of Vietnamese descent. He informed me that his nephew had just come out. He loved the teenager but was afraid for him. How to comfort and protect him? Since he wasn't himself homosexual, my friend turned to me, asking me about my experience as a gay Asian man. All at once, I was drowning in sadness, in melancholy. It all came back. I would've liked to be optimistic, reassuring. To tell him that everything would be fine, that his nephew would live in a world free from hatred and rejection. That his sexual orientation would not occasion any violence. That his ethnic identity would in no way influence the construction of his own individuality or his relations with others. But I didn't say any of that. I found myself unable to predict a thing. It would be up to him to make his own way. I could only hope for the best. That tomorrow's world would prove kinder, more merciful. That he would not go through what I had. That for him, it would get better.

But upon closer inspection, had it all really been that bad for me? Was it true that all I ever did was suffer, passive and powerless, with no control over anything, coming away with no lessons learned? Hadn't I had pivotal encounters, known periods of joy, experienced bliss? Vital as it is to show the dark side of the rainbow, there are shards and glimmers of brilliance to behold.

I think of my own family, scattered across the far-flung corners of the world, with whom I'm not in touch. Among my many nephews and second cousins, there must have been some who realized they were queer. If one of them were to come to me seeking support and comfort, what would I tell them?

Epilogue

For my fortieth birthday, L. bought me a trip to the paradisiacal Cambodian islands in the Gulf of Thailand. We were supposed to spend a few days in the port city of Sihanoukville to ring in the new year, 2021. Though my parents had been living there since moving back to their native land, I didn't go there often, my last visit dating back to over a year before. L. hadn't been for almost a decade, but he'd met them then. When he'd stayed the night, my father had taken care to put us up in separate rooms as far apart from one another as possible, and had been very standoffish with L. As usual, my mother had pretended to be clueless as to what was really going on. This time, we'd booked a hotel just for us, an impressive thirty-floor complex facing the sea with garish slot machines, luxury restaurants, and a newly opened heliport. The city was unrecognizable. The former seaside resort had transformed into a giant construction site open to the heavens, skyscrapers and casinos as far as the eye could see.

It had been several long months since L. and I had seen each other. After I'd left France, the Covid-19 pandemic spread throughout the entire world, putting a halt to international travel. Several months of fear and anxiety, six thousand miles apart. At long last, after countless hurdles and checkpoints, he'd finally been able to join me. In Phnom Penh, but not Taipei. With the pandemic, the job I'd been offered had been redefined. It was no longer about developing cultural projects in the region, but fundraising to ensure the organization's survival. This was what we'd all been reduced to. While the whole world was shaken by the cataclysm, I pondered my own circumstances and my deepest desires. Was it still about enjoying the comfort provided by a job I wasn't really so fond of any more? I resigned but stayed in Cambodia, provoking surprise and incomprehension. *People all over are losing their jobs, and you're being choosy! You've been dreaming about Taiwan for so long! Why didn't you take their part-time offer? At least you'd be able to do something else on the side!* How to tell them that I wanted to make room for what might come my way, without knowing exactly what that was?

The pandemic wasn't the only crisis making its way around. Crises social, racial, and otherwise raged across the continents, and France was by no means spared. If the #MeToo movement came to light in the wake of the Harvey Weinstein affair and Black Lives Matter rallies took on a far larger scope after the murder of George Floyd, it was literature that lit the powder keg in France. Vanessa Springora's *Consent: A Memoir* and Camille Kouchner's *The Familia Grande* had sent shock waves through society and helped promote more open discussion of sexual abuse and incest. As for #metoogay, it made its first appearance after an allegation of rape on Twitter. Testimonials about violence on the gay scene began to emerge. Upon reading the article 'In Search of #MeTooGay,'[13] I shivered:

---

13 Matthieu Foucher, 'À la recherche du #MeTooGay' [In search of the gay #MeToo], *Vice*, 29 September 2020: https://bit.ly/3XQnpXq.

On apps and in gathering places alike, talk is blunt, come-ons upfront, action swift, the issue of consent below the radar, and aggression all too common. And although relationships of dominance and dependence informed by gender aren't the same for hetero- and homosexuals, the latter are far from being innocent of such abuses, and indeed the risk can be increased by factors in the expression of gender, age, race, coloniality, social status, and disability within gay identity.

My own story suddenly took on a new meaning. Perhaps it was my turn to speak? Perhaps it was time no longer to be held back by fear and shame, to rid myself of these at last, once and for all. There was so much to tell. Perhaps I still had things to say?

*

In my parents' cottage, a veritable feast is being prepared: steamed shrimp, spicy crab, fish with ginger. My mother, who's just received an artificial hip, is having trouble moving but insists on setting the table and running the show. L. sits down beside me. My father, garrulous and good-humoured, ventures: *Do you play ping pong? How about a game later?* My mother turns to me and murmurs: *It might be time to think about having children now. Children are the true happiness in life.*